Hidden Disabilities and Conditions

Hidden Disabilities and Conditions

Creating an Inclusive Workplace

Ted Smith

UKHR.com Ltd

Valentina Rinaldi

CONTENTS

CONTENTS

Dedication

This book is dedicated to four very special people: Liz Henson, Sarah McGuinness, Tilley Milburn and Eileen Thornton. Each of them plays a key role in either ensuring that the stigma of hidden disabilities and conditions is challenged and rethought or in promoting the cause amongst HR and Wellbeing practitioners.

All the profits from this book will go to the amazing Macmillan Cancer Support charity, whose website is second to none, and can be found at https://www.macmillan.org.uk/

Introduction

Following publication of my first book, *Human Resources A to Z: A Practical Field Guide for People Managers* (2020), it soon became apparent that there was a need for a second practical guide, this one highlighting disabilities and conditions that often remain hidden in the workplace, but should nevertheless be factored in to the monitoring of the health and wellbeing of all employees. The prevalence of hidden disabilities and conditions cannot be underestimated: in the UK, one in five people have a disability, and eighty per cent of these disabilities are not obvious to others.

Human Resources A to Z contained several chapters on diversity and inclusion that sparked considerable interest and debate. Diversity is vital to all organisations. Creativity, productivity and connection with the community thrive in diverse organisations. Diversity is achieved through inclusion. Create an environment that is welcoming and open for all, where adjustments are made willingly, and people will grow and develop, with productivity levels increasing. Build and sustain such an organisation, and you will enter a virtuous circle. You'll be able to attract, recruit and retain the very best personnel, and the people who use your services, or buy your goods, will keep coming back for more.

By definition, diversity covers many aspects of human life. This book is based upon interviews with people who have a hidden disability or condition, and focuses on practical ideas to make it easier for them to enjoy and feel included in the work environment.

Please do consider including hidden disability awareness in your diversity and unconscious bias training; don't just rest on gender and race. A common frustration of people with unseen conditions is being told 'but you look normal' and having to justify that they have a disability.

Each chapter explains how the person first became aware of their condition, the diagnosis and treatment, and the accommodations that have helped the most. It is written as a resource for HR teams and line managers.

It isn't perfect or complete. Please do send additional ideas and thoughts to 'uktedsmith' on LinkedIn for the second edition.

I suggest that you have a quick skim-through to get an idea of how this book is laid out. Once you have a feel for the contents, dip in and out of the book as needs dictate.

***

Where did my interest in diversity and inclusion (D&I) stem from? I am a straight, privileged white male. My roots are middle class: a liberal father who worked in the public sector and a mother who taught office skills at college. Even though I was born in West Bromwich, I grew up in Shrewsbury and Chelmsford, both reasonably well-to-do towns. All my friends and my teachers were white, and I still remember an early lesson where we were categorically told that white people were more intelligent and civilised than African and Asian people. Shocking, but true.

I was oblivious to the whole field of D&I until I went to study for an environmental science degree at Leicester Polytechnic, and witnessed blatant homophobia and racism for the first time. I felt the injustice of it, and offered my services to both GaySoc and the Afro-Caribbean Society (ACS). This led to paid sabbatical work as an elected Vice President and then President of the Students' Union. I got involved in the Campaign for Disarmament (CND), the Entertainments Committee, Rag Week (student charity fundraiser) and *PRUNE* (the student newspaper), and worked towards harmony between the different ethnic groups. At that time, inclusivity wasn't a word in my vocabulary; I just wanted to help redress the balance. I remember being criticised for approving Linton Kwesi Johnson, a Jamaican dub poet, as an act to appear at the poly; my faith was restored when he not only sold out but the ACS volunteered to provide free security.

Being responsible for forty-five staff, shops, bars, cafés, gigs, parties, travel and insurance centres, as well as frequent liaison with the polytechnic authorities, all at the age of twenty, gave me the confidence to apply for a range of jobs when I left. I chose HR over science after realising that I worked well in that space.

A year as President of the Students' Union meant that my CV stood out from the many other graduates applying for jobs. My first job was as Trainee Personnel Officer at Wycombe District Council. They covered the costs of taking a Diploma in Personnel Management which, in part, made up for the dire wages.

I then found a job in a commercial market research company in Oxford, before a spell in a more senior role at a market research company in Ealing. I saw a job advertised in the *New Scientist* as a chance to combine my love of science and HR with a successful and growing science-based company, GlaxoSmithKline, in Greenford. In my fourteen years there I was involved with two major mergers; undertook a significant culture change project, working alongside experts like Dave Ulrich and Lynda Gratton; learned how to lead progressively larger teams; and took part in some impressive development programmes at INSEAD, Duke and London Business School.

After leaving GSK, I turned down some bigger corporate roles to spend time with my young sons. I joined a small biotech called RiboTargets, which later became Vernalis. There I helped build a vibrant and productive culture with some of the best scientists from a range of international backgrounds. During this time the issues of diversity and inclusion were never far from my mind and I worked to improve the conditions for all employees, regardless of race, gender, sexual preference or disability.

I then spent five years at the Medical Research Council, where I introduced the concept of wellbeing at work and changed their pay and grading systems so that the scientists and technicians were better rewarded for the amazing jobs they did. After this, I spent three years at Wellcome Trust, where I established staff representative meetings, helped set up a major £5m Diversity and Inclusion project, introduced mental health first aiders and made a series of improvements to the layout and use of the building. I worked with researchers in Africa and Asia, and introduced a new training programme for scientists to develop as managers, using an online suite specially developed with the Open University.

Recently, I have worked as a consultant in human resources, organisation development and design, supporting smaller companies. I have enjoyed using my spare time to chair a charity called The Ideas Foundation, which works with young people from disadvantaged backgrounds, and helps them discover their creativity and develop their confidence. This followed periods as a non-exec Trustee at Wysing Arts and many years as Chair of Herts Careers Service.

In summary, I'm a consultant best known for my creativity, focusing on productivity and the development of people. I have broad experience in business strategy, culture change, team leadership, and mergers and acquisitions in private and public sectors covering Europe, the US, Africa and Asia. I've led major strategic reviews concerning culture, information technology and research management, succession planning and talent retention. I've given presentations on the war for talent, culture change and life/work balance in both Europe and the States. I've coached senior board execs, managers and trainees, and mentored way too many people to count. And I've built, rebuilt and learned how to motivate HR and OD professionals whilst keeping stakeholders and budget providers onside.

Much of the inspiration for this book has come from the readers of my articles on LinkedIn and those who continue to ask me questions through my *Dear Ted* blog. If you don't find the answer to your question in this book, then come and find me on LinkedIn by searching for uktedsmith. I'll spend time with you (at no cost to you) discussing your issue, and then I will post a generic answer for others afterwards. And if you don't find me there, then you'll find me at festivals, live sports and gigs, travelling in my camper van or stopping off at the odd real ale festival (when pandemics allow!).

Section A: Accommodations

In this book, the term 'accommodations' refers to any changes in the work environment or how things are done that enable an individual with a disability or a condition to enjoy equal employment opportunities and, more importantly, feel included and part of the team.

Some costs associated with making accommodations can be recovered in the UK through the Access to Work scheme (similar programmes exist in other countries). It is worth finding out what is available at the earliest point, as sometimes costs cannot be retrospectively reclaimed; they have to be approved in advance. Whatever the price, if you ask your colleague what is needed, listen and respond. This will ensure they feel supported and included. If you do some research and find some added extras, you will become a legend.

Further Resources
https://www.gov.uk/access-to-work
https://businessdisabilityforum.org.uk/
https://inclusionscotland.org/
https://stickmancommunications.co.uk/
https://www.theinclusioninitiative.co.uk/
http://hydesmith.com/de-stress/files/StressMgt.pdf

Section B: Creating an Inclusive Environment

Why Bother?

There are several good reasons, but the most important is the simplest: because it is the right thing to do.

Suppose you have someone who is diagnosed with a condition or who lets you know about a disability during the interview process. Why wouldn't you want to make the possibility of them working with you, at their maximum productivity, a reality?

When you make an accommodation for a disability or a condition, you are not just helping that individual feel included in the team, able to work more effectively and efficiently, but you are also sending a message to the rest of the team that you are a caring, thoughtful and responsible employer. Once this message is communicated to the outside world, you will see an increasing number of great people want to come and work with you. This is evidenced by the success seen in universities seeking new staff before and after gaining an Athena SWAN Award for their gender inclusivity.

If you decide not to invest any time or resources in making accommodations, then you might be challenged legally if the affected person can show that you have not made sufficient effort to accommodate their needs. Far worse, you will develop a reputation for being unnecessarily tight, and therefore less of a prospect to work for. You will struggle to recruit the best people, and retaining your current team may become problematic.

Let's assume that you do make the necessary accommodations. The return on your investment will be access to a different way of thinking, increased creativity, higher levels of productivity and the probability of generating greater loyalty.

Whilst there is limited evidential peer-reviewed research that we can call on, anecdotal evidence suggests that organisations who encourage and develop a diverse group of employees and are supportive and open in their recruitment not only end up with high-performing teams, but also achieve a greater connection with their customer base (who are increasingly demanding about matters of social responsibility and environment when making procurement decisions). With some of the big investment funds now asking about these matters, you may even have something significant to add to your annual report, especially if you work in a publicly listed company.

The best employers offer accommodations to all their team members, not just those who require them. Flexible hours, the opportunity to work at home, job sharing and ergonomic or sit/stand workstations are all quite modest in their cost, but provide substantial benefits to the recipients.

Recruitment Adverts

How do we attract a diverse and talented group of people to apply for the position that we have in mind? How do we ensure that they can give their best at the interview or in any part of the application process that we use? To be truly inclusive, we have to start well before the person joins the team.

Some organisations fail at the very first step. They use language in their adverts that discourages or even stops people from applying. I am not referring to the blatant discrimination seen in adverts that state someone has to be male or female (without a reason being given), but to the more subtle use of macho or aggressive language.

Using previous academic research from The University of Waterloo and Duke University, which outlined a series of male and female gender-coded words, Total Jobs analysed 76,000 UK job adverts over six weeks to assess the frequency of gender-coded words in UK recruitment. They found more than 470,000 words that carried gender bias: an average of six male-coded or female-coded words per job advert.

The leading examples of male-gendered words included: Lead (over 70,000 mentions); Analyse (35,000); Competitive (23,000); Active (20,000); and Confident (nearly 14,000).

They found that most commonly used female-gendered words in UK job descriptions included: Support (83,000); Responsible (65,000); Understanding (nearly 30,000); Dependable (17,000); and Committed (13,000).

Looking at different sectors, they found that some were more gendered than others: Social care (87% female bias); Secretarial/Admin (67% female bias); Cleaning (62% female bias); Housekeeping (77% female bias); Science (62% male bias); Sales (51% male bias vs 35% female bias); and Marketing (52% male bias vs 33% female bias).

To be aware of potential bias, Total Jobs offers a free decoder:
https://www.totaljobs.com/insidejob/gender-bias-decoder/

Aside from trying to write an advert that is not gender biased, the next issue is to show that you are an inclusive organisation. Many say, often somewhat glibly, that they recruit regardless of gender, religion, etc. and are equal opportunities employers, but the ones that have attempted to do something about it shine out by adding some extra affiliations. Good examples might include a commitment to the Disability Confident Scheme or the Stonewall Diversity Champions programme.

Thought also needs to be given to where the adverts will run. Examine the readership of the media you are using to ensure that your vacancy will be accessed by a diverse set of people. Is that local paper or website truly seen by all members of the local community? Beware of recruiting through word of mouth alone; you can end up recruiting a homogenous group of similar-minded people.

Disability Confident Scheme

In the UK, the government provides a scheme to show applicants that an employer supports initiatives to help people with disabilities enter the workforce and retain roles within it. It runs over three levels.

The first level is 'Disability Confident Committed', in which employers demonstrate that they have inclusive and accessible recruitment practices, that they are inclusively communicating vacancies, are offering interviews to disabled people and providing reasonable adjustments, as well as supporting existing employees.

Level 2 is called 'Disability Confident Employer'. It requires self-assessment around two themes: 'Getting the right people for your business' and 'Keeping and developing your people'. Disability Confident Employers 'are recognised as going the extra mile to make sure disabled people get a fair chance'.

Level 3 is the 'Disability Confident Leader', which requires the employer to become a champion within their local or sector communities. This level requires that the self-assessment is validated by someone outside the business, a narrative to show what is being done to support the status as a Disability Confident Leader and confirmation that the organisation is employing disabled people.

Interviews

'We understand that interviews can be difficult for some people who live with a condition or disability. We want to make it as easy as possible for every candidate to shine during their interview, so please let us know what we can do to accommodate you.'

Phrases like this, included with an invitation to interview, can help someone decide to talk about their needs and potentially give a better interview. When someone responds with a request, take time to listen and see how you can best respond. In some cases, you might need to allow someone extra time to complete tests. In other cases, you might need to arrange an interview for the late morning to allow the person to comfortably get to the meeting, or provide assurance that there are no steps or obstacles between the drop-off point or car park and the interview room. Some candidates may need the offer of toilet facilities on arrival or to bring a supporter with them.

To save any possible embarrassment, I always assume that people prefer to use the lift for interviews in a building with multiple floors. Even if they have no hidden condition or visible disability, they won't feel that they have to keep pace with me on the stairs and get stressed about getting out of breath in the process. If the job requires a medical (e.g. for a warehouse role), leave it to the doctors rather than trying to invent your own physical tests!

In one interview that I arranged, the candidate had explained that she could only sit for about twenty minutes before she needed to move around. We held several fifteen-minute sessions in the room to discuss sensitive issues and about twenty minutes walking slowly around the building whilst chatting.

I've twice been in an interview situation where the interviewee has become so overwhelmed by the enormity of the event that they have completely frozen and been unable to speak. For the first, I suggested that we go and get a coffee, and for the second, that we go for a walk outside the building. Both candidates were fine after being reassured.

Where there is a panel interview and a presentation is going off the rails, don't watch the train crash: intervene and reboot. Take the candidate out of the room, and give them a chance to recompose themselves (close out the feed temporarily if interviewing remotely). Remind the panel that it could be any one of them and that you have created an artificial environment loaded with stress, quite unlike the normal workplace. Explain to the candidate that you want them to be able to give their best, and that you respect the fact they are so passionate about working for you, then start again from the beginning.

Whatever you do will be appreciated and will help the person return to and re-engage with the interview, which can be stressful for everyone, let alone for those with a condition.

Starting Work
Sometimes people do not disclose a condition before they accept a job. This is because they fear that by being open and honest, they will not get selected. If they disclose after acceptance, then your role is to listen and understand the nature of the disability or condition, how it affects them and the sort of accommodations that will need to be made before they start work.

The line manager needs to take responsibility for the new employee, but there can be help from a range of people in human resources, occupational health, security, facilities and IT to get everything set up.

In Work
For many of the people interviewed for this book, their hidden disability or condition was diagnosed whilst they were in active employment. Having had to take time out for clinic appointments, tests and the like, the

point at which they make their disclosure needs to be treated with calm and reason. For some, the accommodations needed are relatively simple and can be resolved by the line manager in conjunction with their HR Business Partner, but occasionally the changes will be more profound and will include referral to occupational health, with appropriate support from Facilities and IT where changes to the physical layout, computer hardware or software are needed.

Whatever policies and procedures are in place, you should always respond quickly to an accommodation request, keep the person informed about the status of their request and, once implemented, ensure a regular review.

Occasionally, providing support to someone can rebound on you as other employees ask why they are getting perceived preferential treatment.

'Why is Kallik allowed to work at home when we can't?'

'I want a sit-stand desk and super rolling mouse like Kallik's.'

You will have to make your own judgement call on these knock-on effects. On some occasions (working hours especially), it might be that the current policies and practices need to be changed for all. In other cases (e.g. relatively expensive equipment), it may be that you hold the line that they will be provided upon the recommendation of the occupational health team or a doctor.

Leaving Work

Most organisations carry out some form of exit interview when people leave. This can be an excellent opportunity to learn from someone with a disability or condition, as their departure may make them feel more open to giving positive and negative criticism. Ask, listen and learn. Simple!

Company Benefits Programmes

Organisations can provide some amazing benefits to their employees at a fraction of the cost to individuals by buying into group schemes. These benefit schemes not only provide a good level of protection, intervention and support; they also act as an important part of the total reward package, aiding in candidate attraction and team retention too.

Schemes include Group Pension, which has to be offered in the UK (401k plans in the US), Life Assurance, Income Protection (also known as sick pay insurance) and Private Medical Insurance. Additions include Employee Assistance Programmes (EAP, sometimes EAR – Employee Advisory Resource), Cash Plans, dental, optical and travel insurance.

Where finances are tight and employee benefits are considered a luxury, an EAP scheme can offer exceptionally good value for money. Internet or phone-based, they cost as little as a few pounds per employee per year. For tens of pounds, you can buy more comprehensive services that include counselling, legal support, debt advice, and health and wellbeing support. Most employers will find that these schemes quickly pay for themselves in terms of productivity. Not having to worry about a parking ticket, sourcing a great nursery school locally for the children, or resolving a dispute with a neighbour can be a huge relief, let alone the chance to talk about a major relationship breaking down with a counsellor.

With a higher budget, a Group Income Protection scheme will provide a percentage of pay to employees who cannot work due to illness or injury. They usually come with full support around rehabilitation case management, a fully-fledged EAP, as well as health and wellbeing support and initiatives. The rehabilitation case management service assesses an individual's health condition, providing support and advice to the employer, recommendations for reasonable adjustments to the role, return to work plans, and even recommendations for treatment (such as physio and counselling), which will expedite a return to work.

Private Medical Insurance (PMI) speeds the return to full productivity by helping the employee access healthcare without the lengthy waiting lists inherent in the NHS system. They can provide services such as online 24/7 GP services, second medical opinions from specialists, as well as muscular-skeletal and cancer support pathways. Some provide incentivisation for healthier lifestyles habits, such as physical exercise or mindfulness, via smartwatch tracking, with points earned for healthy behaviours. Look carefully at their provisions for cancer and dementia; some are very limited. Also worth noting is the phrase, 'medical history disregarded', which means that a new employee with a pre-existing condition will be covered. 'Moratorium' underwriting excludes all pre-existing conditions from the last five years for a set period, usually two years, but may then include them after that. There could also be a deferred period before a new employee is able to claim. You never know when someone will become ill; it could be on day two of their employment. Not everyone waits the necessary six months stipulated in their offer letter, so take this into consideration!

It is short of complete PMI, yet Benenden and others are viable alternatives, especially for smaller companies. In essence, these programmes ask you to start with your NHS doctor and consultant, and they only intervene if treatment is delayed beyond a trigger period. It's fall-back insurance against a lengthy wait, and depending on the level of cover chosen, it can also include physio and counselling, in addition to fast-track surgery.

Critical Illness Cover is a more limited variant that tends to be sold to individuals rather than companies. However, it can be offered in the suite of benefits available. It provides a lump-sum payment on the diagnosis of a condition, which will be stipulated in the provider's list of health conditions that are covered.

Another variant is Key Person Cover, sometimes purchased by organisations that fear the effect of the death or serious illness of a critical member of their team. Depending upon the policy, it can cover the costs of hiring an interim replacement, or in some cases, the loss of profit that results from them not being present.

In addition to providing schemes, many organisations try to give some flexibility. These flexible benefits programmes (cafeteria benefits in the USA) reduce universal paternalistic provision and give the employee a choice between plans to reflect their current circumstances. A young person living at home, for example, may choose to reduce their life insurance in exchange for extreme sports protection. There are many such choices to be made.

A good employee benefits consultancy can advise on all the options: analyse your employee's needs, propose a framework, find partners and providers to deliver the best solutions for you, then constantly review its effectiveness and value for money. And, as a final tip, don't just negotiate on the price per employee; see what extras you can get as well (reporting functionality, reductions in excess insurance costs, added services such as tailored apps, reduced moratorium, counselling provision, etc).

Blue Badge Parking Scheme and Sunflower Lanyards

In the UK, people with a disability can apply for a blue badge from their county council that allows them to park in a disabled parking bay. The scheme's eligibility criteria include people who cannot walk without considerable psychological distress or risking serious harm. In other words, the person does not need to be wheelchair-bound to have a blue badge.

The expansion of the scheme has led to problems at supermarket car parks, where someone getting out of their car and walking to the shop without the use of a chair or walking frame has been accused of abusing the right to park. The issue, of course, is that the disability might be hidden and yet very real in terms of the need for the person to be able to park near the store entrance.

This is why some people prefer to wear a sunflower lanyard, a symbol that explains to shopworkers and others that they have a hidden disability or condition. https://hiddendisabilitiesstore.com/ gives details about the UK lanyard scheme.

Section C: Working with GPs, Doctors, Consultants, Health Insurance and Occupational Health

Doctors undertake five years at medical school before choosing to spend a further five to ten years training in a specific field. There are many choices to be made, from working as a specialist in a hospital (anaesthesiology, gynaecology, radiology, paediatrics, etc), to becoming a generalist in accident and emergency, intensive care or working as a general practitioner in the community. All these roles and many more are key to a successful healthcare system.

To access healthcare, most people start with a GP and typically are either prescribed medicines or counselling, or obtain a referral to a specialist. Some bypass this phase altogether by entering the hospital following an emergency.

GPs – known as general community health care doctors in other countries – do a difficult job. In their ten years of training, they try to understand as much as possible about the human body, from babies to the elderly, and then attend regular, continuous professional development courses and conferences after qualifying.

When a patient goes to see their GP, it is often because something is proving difficult to live with. They are either ill or in pain, and often both. The GP has an allotted amount of time per patient and is skilled at asking questions to try to work out whether the issue can be treated with painkillers, antibiotics, antidepressants, or needs counselling or a specialist referral.

Unfortunately, the majority of the people that I interviewed for this book have not had a good experience with their GP, and several also had issues with not being taken seriously at a specialist referral. All have gone on to be diagnosed with long-term conditions. This finding is concerning, and it warrants careful consideration and preparation unless you have private healthcare or the funds to self-refer.

The GP

A GP has a list of patients to see or call and a finite amount of time to deal with them. They do not have the time to listen to a life story or a wide range of symptoms. They are trained to get quickly to the main cause. If you present with a high temperature, they will seek the cause; the same with pain. Rarely will they consider more than two symptoms at once; they will take the one that is causing the most distress and concentrate on that. In so doing, they are missing a trick; they are not looking at the patient from a holistic perspective but as a physically ill person needing treatment.

Many times GPs will prescribe medicines and suggest that the patient should only return if the presenting issue is not resolved by the time the prescription concludes. Many interviewees reported that when they returned, their prescription was simply doubled (40mg per day instead of 20mg, for example), and they were sent on their way again. In several cases, women were told that they should expect pain with their periods and get on with life 'like everyone else'. Much later they would receive a specialist diagnosis of endometriosis.

One of my interviewees was sent to their local phlebotomy service for a series of blood tests. When the tests came back negative, she was told that it was probably 'just hormonal' and to up the painkillers until her hormone levels balanced. She was diagnosed with cancer a few months later.

Children of interviewees accentuate the point. Parents have been told that they will 'grow out of their condition' (it turned out to be a rare genetic disorder), 'it's just a phase' (it was actually the early signs of Tourette's), and 'I understand that parents sometimes over-react' (the hay fever that the GP diagnosed that later that evening required a nebuliser in hospital for acute asthma).

One interviewee was told not to worry because all they had was a trapped nerve. Their condition turned out to be multiple sclerosis, which might have been diagnosed earlier if all the symptoms had been reviewed at the same time. So be prepared to trust your instincts, stand your ground when you need to and request a second opinion.

From bitter experience, the following suggestions have been made repeatedly by my interviewees:

- Keep a diary, or a log, of *all* the symptoms that you are experiencing and the medical practitioners that you meet along the way. Sometimes one extra symptom can help swing a diagnosis (especially for something like lupus), so don't hold back. Either print it out, or make sure the handwriting is clearly legible, and hand a copy to your GP. If you have any pre-existing conditions (e.g. you are on pills to regulate blood pressure), note them down as well as your age, weight and height. Your GP may be so pressed for time that they haven't been able to access your notes before seeing you, or their IT system may be playing up.
- Take a relative or friend with you (called an advocate) if you want moral support. Agree with them in advance on what it is that you want to try to resolve at the appointment. You may forget things in the moment, but your advocate is there to remind you.
- Do some simple research on the internet. Do not assume that you have every disease that the internet suggests! In more complex cases (e.g. if you know that you have something like leukaemia), read the NICE guidelines and see what you would expect to receive (e.g. some counselling in addition to treatment). Know your rights. Sometimes a GP surgery is pressed for budget and doesn't want to refer everyone to specialists towards the end of the financial year.

If you have stood your ground, had a second opinion, but still feel that something is seriously wrong, then write a formal letter of complaint so that your case can be reviewed by an independent practitioner. This has worked wonders with three of my interviewees.

Initial Diagnosis
Once you know what your condition is, it is well worth reviewing the NHS website, which is a mine of information. Also consult the NICE

website for your condition to understand what you are entitled to in the UK. Review charity websites that specialise in your condition. There are often Facebook and Instagram patient groups, but remember that these are unregulated and can be quite unnerving to read, as people try to claim they have the worst possible case of whatever it is!

Remember that Jacinda, from down the street, is genetically different to you. Even if she has had a similar diagnosis, the treatment regime might need to be different for you. Avoid taking action on the basis of hearsay. Rely instead on informed opinion.

The Specialist/Consultant

Listening to my interviewees, it seems that consultants ignore the notes made by the GP and start their own diagnosis from scratch. They are specialists, and their job is to see what they can do in their field to make your life more comfortable. The best will look holistically at all your symptoms, ask about your lifestyle and attempt to work out whether medicines, counselling or surgery are appropriate. Sometimes they will suggest that you should see another specialist, e.g. your back pain results from a gynaecological condition, which requires an endocrinologist to review, rather than their musculoskeletal expertise.

Take your log/diary of symptoms with you and show them a copy. It will help them get up to speed fast and will often carry more weight than the brief introductory letter they will have received from the referring doctor.

The Counsellor or Mental Health Team

When a life-changing condition has been diagnosed, the NICE guidelines propose that the patient is referred to counselling or mental health support. This can be essential to help you come to terms with the condition, resolve your anger, rethink your life plans or simply restart your new life.

Some referrals for counselling are driven by guidelines and yet can be interpreted differently by medical practitioners in different geographic areas. Push for what you know that you need. For example, don't allow someone to say that you can only receive counselling for miscarriage after the third event; everyone handles something like this in a different way.

On occasion, counselling is the recommended treatment for mental health conditions, such as anxiety and PTSD. The counsellor, psychiatrist or psychologist will hold a series of sessions over several months, during which all the issues are discussed and reframed. These sessions will often be accompanied by training in a skill, such as cognitive behavioural therapy (CBT).

Listening to my interviewees, these programmes are truly hit or miss. Some have had successful interventions (often alongside prescription drugs to give their minds space to work, with antidepressants the drug of choice). But sometimes the interventions are low grade, and as one person said, 'Breathing exercises alone will not help me with my anxiety'.

If you receive the appropriate support, it will help you come to terms with your condition and learn to control it better. If the treatment is not working after several sessions, go back and ask to be re-assessed. Only you know your own mind and body. Only you can be your own advocate in such circumstances.

Occupational Health (OH)

When working with an occupational health specialist, consultancy, agency or referral service, start by finding out their qualifications and areas of expertise. Some will have covered a basic-level diploma, achieved online, that enables them to advise on topics like the ergonomics of working spaces, whilst others will have trained as a doctor at medical school and then specialised in workplace medicine. Even though their training, qualifications and number of years spent learning may be dramatically different, they might still call themselves occupational health consultants. Sometimes you will need to seek an OH specialist in the field that you are investigating rather than rely on the person who predominantly carries out your DSE (Display Screen Equipment) or pre-employment checks.

Once you have established the level of support you are accessing, you can work with them to provide the best set of accommodations for the condition or disability that has been diagnosed. A good OH provider will give sensible advice on return to work and hours building back up to full time, in addition to ideas for IT and Facilities solutions to make the workplace more accessible by the person with the condition.

Section D: Common (Non-Medicine-Based) Treatments

Aside from prescribed medicines, there is a small number of non-chemical treatments that provide support for a relatively large number of disabilities and conditions. These are briefly reviewed below. Please note this is a lay person's guide only, and actual clinical practice varies between specialists and countries.

Counselling

Counselling provides people with the opportunity to talk about their feelings and emotions with a trained therapist. The counsellor uses techniques to help the person feel at ease and talk about all their issues in a safe environment without being judged or criticised.

Counselling is commonly offered by GPs through referral for mental health conditions, such as depression, anxiety or eating disorders; a physical health condition that is causing stress or deep unhappiness, such as infertility or lupus; or issues related to relationships, self-confidence, work-related stress or gender identity. A trained therapist will help the person understand their own feelings and thought processes, but they will not usually provide solutions.

Mindfulness

Some people struggle with wave after wave of negative thoughts entering their minds, often related to anxiety about events that may or may not occur. Mindfulness is a series of techniques in which people learn to focus on what they are sensing and feeling in the moment, without interpretation or judgment. Practising mindfulness involves breathing methods and other exercises to relax both the body and the mind, reduce stress and allow the person to either move on with the tasks they need to achieve or get to sleep.

Cognitive Behavioural Therapy (CBT)

When diagnosed or living with a condition or disability, many people find themselves trapped in a spiral of negative thoughts. All the issues, problems and changed life circumstances that they are faced with can be overwhelming. The chance to be heard through counselling, or practising mindfulness, is sufficient for many, but sometimes additional support is required.

CBT is based on the concept that a person's thoughts, feelings, physical sensations and actions are interconnected, and that negative thoughts and feelings can become a vicious cycle. CBT aims to help the person deal with overwhelming problems in a more positive way by breaking them down into smaller parts, and provides a framework to change the negative patterns. It looks for practical ways to improve the state of mind on a daily basis, and once taught, it can be used as regularly as needed.

Section E: The Impact of a Hidden Disability or Condition on an Individual

Mental Health

A common thread across most of the interviews that I have conducted, and the papers that I have read, is that the diagnosis of a hidden disability or condition often gives a temporary feeling of euphoria: at long last, the doctors have decided what is happening, given it a name and treatment can commence. The individual can search and find all sorts of information, join social media groups and chat to fellow patients about the best medications, changes to lifestyle and ways to get appropriate support, depending upon which country they live in.

Unfortunately, that euphoria is short-lived, as they are hit with the realisation that they will be dependent upon drugs, treatments, physiotherapy or counselling for many years to come. They may have to make substantial changes to their lifestyle regarding jobs, families, holidays, trips, even where they live. One of the hardest things to accept is they are no longer the same person they were before everything started. The realisation for many is gradual; a slow erosion of opportunities. For others, it hits them like a freight train.

The best doctors and consultants are aware of the impact of diagnosing a long-term health condition. They make immediate arrangements for appropriate therapy or counselling, to reduce the mental health impact. Others only provide additional support when pushed, so HR and Occupational Health teams need to step in and fill the gap.

The most reported issue is tiredness. Trying to get to sleep when the brain is trying to process all the newly acquired information is tough. Tiredness builds up over time and can lead to additional illness as the body becomes prone to bacterial and viral infection. It also affects work and home life. Many tell me that they started forgetting simple things and had to write lists to keep on top of everything.

As the enormity of the diagnosis takes its toll, depression affects a smaller number of people (ten per cent in my sample). Depression can lead to additional medication such as antidepressants and sleeping tablets, and further complications. Many have found alternatives to medication, the most popular being mindfulness and associated activities like yoga. Sadly, others have turned to alcohol and other avoidance measures.

Often, the opportunity to simply discuss the issue is most helpful. The popularity of specialist disease and condition-related Facebook groups has grown exponentially in the past few years, and gives people the chance to discuss their issues, treatments, current research and provide help to one another. They do need to be handled carefully, though. The comments are rarely moderated and can contain poor advice, as well as hosting competitive and combative personality types.

Financial Health

Living with a long-term condition can have a series of financial consequences, and it is important that these are recognised by HR teams and are not exacerbated.

The first consequence that many of my interviewees have suffered is that they have seen a reduction in their take-home pay. When they challenge their HR team, they discover that their three visits in three weeks (to the GP, consultant and then a scan) automatically tripped a move to basic sick pay, pending a review of their case. HR teams must find ways to remove, or at least reduce, this impact. It is difficult enough discovering that you have a long-term health issue without having to fight for your pay. These automated absence systems certainly have a role to play, but they need a human steer.

The eye-opening costs of having a condition reported to me include:

- Pay: lost overtime, lost basic pay, reduced bonuses.
- Travel: for those who can still drive, clinic car parks are a nightmare. Many ask you to buy the hours you need upfront, but you have no idea how long the appointment will take. For those unable to drive,

the combination of buses, trains, tubes and taxis is expensive and often adds extra time to the journey. Alternatively, reliance on friends to provide lifts brings an extra burden of gratitude, requiring flowers or other gifts as a thank you.

- Prescription medicines: one person was paying over £70 pcm until she was introduced to the pre-paid prescription certificate and later a free prescription service after her final diagnosis.
- Many painkillers, creams and ointments are not covered by the NHS. One person spends between £50 and £70 pcm on migraine strips, essential skin creams, ibuprofen and paracetamol. Another spends more than this on absorbent towels for her heavy bleeding. Another has bought cold caps and hair clips, varying in price. Some asthma inhalers and blood-measuring devices have to be privately financed.
- Counselling: people reported that they either received three or six sessions with the NHS and then had to turn to private support, at between £50 and £100 per session. Some got extra support from their company EAR (employee advisory resource), but not many.
- Physio and massage: whilst some physio treatments are included, people with certain conditions need additional support and have to pay between £25 and £50 per session, just to keep their muscles working properly.
- House modifications: aside from some small government grants and disability grants, most modifications to housing have to be self-financed.
- Childcare: with a range of clinic and hospital appointments to attend, someone has to look after the children, often at a cost.
- Tech: working at home whilst unwell or in a clinic waiting room drove some people to buy their own iPads or similar to stay connected. (Please note some of the interviews for this book took place pre-Covid, and certain appointments may no longer require physical attendance due to advances in technology and remote working.)
- Diet: some conditions require specific diets, which can prove to be more expensive, especially if the rest of the family is eating differently.

- Holidays: often, annual leave has to be used for appointments at clinics, meaning that the person doesn't have a proper break from work unless they buy extra leave.
- Travelling abroad: working and/or holidaying abroad can be more expensive if you have to pre-arrange refrigeration for your medicines on the aircraft and at your accommodation. Doctors charge for a letter to take with you to persuade customs officials that the drugs you are carrying are for your personal use.

In 2019 SCOPE carried out extensive research and reported that 'life costs £583 a month more on average if you are disabled'.

Imposter Syndrome

A large number of the people that I interviewed for this book kept apologising for the trouble that they were putting me through to understand their story. As I probed more, I realised that there was a common thread.

Many people with a hidden disability or condition feel as though they are imposters. They don't have a missing limb or other physical disability that is obvious to one and all, and they feel that requesting help is unreasonable. They believe that they should just live with their condition. And that, of course, is exactly what a lot of people do. It is precisely why the statistics at most organisations of the number of people working for them with a disability is lower than it actually is, sometimes by a factor of fifty per cent. Those people never mention their issues and are probably less productive at work as a consequence.

Only by being more open and more welcoming can we become more inclusive. In the same way that some leading organisations are now reducing the stigma of mental health, others must follow with hidden conditions. Once they do, people will be able to be themselves, express themselves and become even more amazing assets of the organisation.

Section F: Hidden Disabilities and Conditions

In 2020 the Office of National Statistics estimated that there were 14.1 million disabled people in the UK (twenty-one per cent of a population of sixty-seven million).

Of the 14.1m disabled people, 1.1m (eight per cent) required the regular use of a wheelchair.

There is a one in six chance that the person next to you in the queue has a disability or condition, even though it is not obvious to you. And this is a conservative estimate.

The following is not an exhaustive list of disabilities and conditions; it covers those that people have been willing to talk to me about. If you have a condition that you would like to appear in the second edition of this book, get in touch with me on LinkedIn by searching for uktedsmith.

1

Anxiety, Stress and Mental Health

Anxiety disorders are complex and rarely easy to resolve, covering many symptoms. Excessive and intrusive worrying is probably the most debilitating; it is disruptive and reduces productivity. Other symptoms include agitation, difficulty concentrating, irritability, restlessness and muscle tensing. Getting to sleep and then sustaining sleep is an issue, which leads to fatigue, and that can make the person susceptible to infection.

One of the factors that can trigger anxiety is stress, which comes from many sources: work deadlines, exams, public speaking, financial worries, personal issues and even world events outside the control of the individual. Anxiety isn't always rational and can be heightened by unhelpful social media or news stories.

A mixture of stress and anxiety can lead to a downturn in mental health. Without the right counselling or medical intervention, it can spiral out of control, so it is one area where you should always seek early help or be signposted to receive it.

As a teenager, Katy's GP was dismissive of her mental health and swept everything under the carpet. Antidepressants would solve all the problems she was told, and this was the pattern through her years at university as well.

She suffered what she describes as ten years of hell, battling anxiety and stress in the working environment. This was at a time when mental health issues were considered a sign of weakness and so had to be kept hidden from managers and colleagues.

Anxiety either creeps up on Katy, or it arrives in a rush. Personal issues can trigger it, but is more often than not related to stress at work created by increasing demands, time-bound projects and the pressure to keep on top of a varied workload. Through trial and error, she has found ways to self-manage her personal issues, such as pursuing her hobby of weightlifting or just simply chatting with supportive friends.

Katy is proud of her workplace, especially about the many changes that have been made to accommodate her and others like her. Rather than the topic of mental health being avoided, as it was in the past, it is now openly discussed, and a series of measures have been taken to make the workplace more inclusive. These have been enhanced as a consequence of the pandemic and reflect the need for so many people to work from home without the direct support of people in the office.

HR Accommodations

Katy suggests that consideration should be given to:

- Talking openly in the workplace about mental health and ways to deal with it. With so many working from home, this means including the subject in catch-up sessions by Zoom or an equivalent. Senior leaders talking about their own mental health helps to ensure that it becomes a normal part of everyday conversation.
- Encouraging flexible working, so that people don't feel under pressure to produce when they are not in a good place.
- Accepting that everyone is different and that there is no single solution for all. If someone says they have an issue with their mental health, the answer shouldn't be assumed. Allowing employees to take the lead in finding the best way forward.
- Providing extended counselling services through the EAP (employee advisory resource) on-demand 24/7, and regularly giving examples of how it can be used.

- Running confidential surveys to check that sufficient support is in place and that line managers are behaving in an appropriate way.
- Setting up a mental health first aider network and collating anonymous statistics from the team to understand the common issues, while pinpointing what needs further work or support.
- Ensuring that HR teams review mental health issues and provision with senior line managers regularly.

Further Resources

www.mentalhealth.org.uk/
www.anxietyuk.org.uk/
www.mhfaengland.org/

2

Aphasia

At its most basic, aphasia is a disorder that affects a person's ability to speak, read, write and/or understand. It is estimated that as many as 350,000 are diagnosed with aphasia in the UK, although not all cases are formally recorded. There are many different types of aphasia with different levels of severity. Some forms are obvious to the observer, but many are hidden. All are linked to a brain injury or trauma, often caused by a stroke or a hit to the head, but sometimes related to an infection that affects the brain.

José had a series of mini-strokes in his brain about three months after receiving chemotherapy for lung cancer. Thankfully the cancer was in remission, so his body could receive the treatment for the mini-strokes (a blood thinner drug). Working with a physiotherapist, he managed to recover his ability to walk and use his hands and arms, but his speech was severely affected.

Initially, a specialist worked with him to improve his swallowing, which was key to eating and drinking properly. Then a speech therapist ran a series of tried and tested routines, but, although his brain was willing, he struggled to get his mouth, tongue and throat to coordinate. He said that he felt just like a drunken schoolboy, slurring uncertainly over a few words and completely failing with others. José's brain remains unaffected. This was a surprise to his doctors and therapists, who assumed he would struggle with comprehension.

Unlike most patients, José never fully recovered his speech. He relies today on a small number of phrases that he has practised many times to be able to say so that ninety-nine per cent of people can understand. He jokes that they are not the phrases that you learn when studying a language, like 'Can you show me the way to the train station?', but instead are those needed for basic survival, such as 'Could you tell me where the toilet is, please?' and 'White and no sugar, please.' When he needs to communicate at a further level, he types onto an iPad with a fold-away keyboard and either shares the screen for people to read or uses the robot voice to read it out. Often he hits the wrong key in the wrong place and has received filthy stares in a theatre after saying that he wanted chocolate-flavoured ice cream just before the interval came!

HR Accommodations

José has been thankful for all the support that he has received from his employer and recommends the following:

- Immediately after the brain trauma, the best support that can be given is sending a clear message that all work is being covered and that your employee shouldn't worry about anything at work, alongside a note or a call to ask how they would like to keep in touch.
- The period of convalescence can be anything between one and six months (for José, this was about four months in total).
- When return to the workplace is discussed, the employee will probably have been briefed by one of their therapists on what to ask for. A phased return to work including travelling outside of the rush hour is standard, together with the resolution of some IT needs (a lightweight laptop or tablet with appropriate text-to-speech software is best).
- Depending upon the type of aphasia diagnosed, there may be limitations to the type of work that the employee can do whilst recovering. José knows fellow patients who have not been able to return to their original jobs and have had to find a suitable alternative. If, for example, their ability to comprehend or understand

complex issues is diminished, or their ability to write complete sentences or phrases is poor, then the response will be very different to a loss of speech or ability to read. Thankfully, there are technological solutions to many problems, and a senior member of the IT team should be included in the support group from an early point.

José was assigned a buddy on return, who accompanied him on tea breaks and to most meetings, helping resolve problems until enough people got to know José's limitations, as well as his many advantages.

Further Resources
https://www.aphasia.org/aphasia-definitions/

See Also
Head Injuries
Hydrocephalus

3

Attention Deficit Hyperactivity
Disorder (ADHD)

ADHD comes in many forms, with varying levels of severity. In some, it is obvious, whilst in others, it is hidden. The linking factor is that most people who are diagnosed have difficulty in concentrating on a subject or task, as well as having to deal with impulsiveness and periods of high levels of activity. It has been found through the use of MRI scanning that they have different structural properties and chemical balances in their brain, resulting in functional problems. Whilst ADHD cannot be 'cured', there is a range of medicines, therapeutic and behavioural interventions that can play a big part in helping control the most difficult aspects of the disorder. Counselling and coaching techniques to reduce the impact of ADHD can play an important part, and many work better with mature patients.

Sue was diagnosed as an adult. Once diagnosed, she felt like a weight was lifted from her shoulders. Many issues that had bothered her throughout her life now fell into place – a welcome development given that she enjoys analysing events in some depth. Sue's diagnosis meant that she could be offered appropriate treatments to help her in her daily life. She has benefitted from the coaching and has also been prescribed methylphenidate hydrochloride and clonidine hydrochloride, which provide some relief. However, a side effect for Sue is appetite suppression, and this has led to work colleagues wrongly assuming she is anorexic, which can be upsetting.

Her disorder frustrates her because her symptoms get in the way of everyday life. She regularly gets locked out of the house or her car by forgetting her keys. She struggles with a trip to the supermarket, getting distracted by all the special offers and the regularity with which goods are moved around the store. She will arrive home with a random set of ingredients that won't make a meal and will have to go back again. One day she set a personal record by having to make five separate trips to get what she needed. Meal planning doesn't happen, and cooking often fails, so her diet can be somewhat hit and miss. Sue writes appointments in her diary and then forgets to look at them. She knows she needs her medication but forgets to order it. And she lives at either full speed or dead stop as a consequence of all these complicating factors.

When life is at full speed, and she is engaged with a subject, Sue is passionate, focused and productive. She describes these as her 'super-woman' moments. She's had some of her best ideas, made some wonderful breakthroughs and felt really good about life, recognising that she has something special to offer.

Sue likes to analyse and reflect, so much so that she says she can get stuck in her own thoughts. This leads to the dead-stop status, where she just needs to stand and stare at a wall (literally) whilst she processes all the data whirring around in her head.

Sue is aware that she can become sensitive when challenged or criticised. This can be particularly difficult in a work setting, and it's here that the impact of ADHD can be profound.

When made to feel included and properly supported, Sue is one of the most productive people in the team, with clarity and insight that goes way beyond the norm. Without the right support, her self-confidence and self-esteem plummet, and she becomes much less productive. Indeed, Sue can be sensitive to any push-back or challenge and becomes angry, losing all focus of the objective at hand.

HR Accommodations

These are Sue's thoughts about how to work with someone who presents with ADHD at work:

- ADHD is a recognised disability and, as such, is a protected characteristic. If you are aware of a candidate with ADHD applying for a role, then you should take appropriate measures to accommodate any reasonable requests for the interview or for work.
- You should show interest by reading about and understanding ADHD; there's lots of material on the internet.
- To be genuinely inclusive as employers, we need to spend time understanding what it is like to be one of the three per cent of the population with ADHD. We shouldn't assume that everyone who has this disorder is either aware that they have it or that they are receiving the correct treatment.
- If the person is required to drive as a part of their role, it may be sensible to refer to Occupational Health for an assessment, and a reasonable adjustment might be the provision of an automatic car.
- Consider providing ongoing coaching support to give the ADHD person an outlet for their emotions if they are triggered.
- Provide a virtual 'time out' card that the person can use when needed to pause what they are doing and regroup.
- When devising away days or team meetings, ensure there are proper breaks for the ADHD folk to pause and reflect. These breaks will also be loved by the introverts.
- When giving feedback, you must set the feedback in context, not simply deliver it head-on. For example, don't mark up a Word document and return it by email: talk it through instead, explaining the background to the issue and why it matters.
- Give feedback in a positive way and show the person a way forward. Negativity will usually backfire.
- If you can, offer a mobile phone number upfront and in advance. It is inevitable that someone in the workplace will say something

inappropriate at some point; if they can phone you and get it out of their system, the sooner, the better.

- Sometimes ADHD people just need space and time to themselves, and sometimes moods can fluctuate during a day. If you can recognise and accept this, things will go well.
- Avoid saying phrases like 'toughen up', 'stop being oversensitive', 'just concentrate on this for now' and 'have you had your meds today?'. Whilst you might mean well, these are likely to go down very badly indeed.
- Believe in them and trust them.
- Accept that there will be errors in their written work. Find a way to take the best bits and enhance them, rather than criticise and make fun of them.
- Be aware that when doing something for the first time, they may feel vulnerable and far more sensitive than usual.
- If they become emotional about something, give them a chance to talk it through with you.
- Sometimes they won't be able to see through the fog of ADHD and will need time to reflect and recover before re-joining you and your team.

Further Resources
https://www.adhdfoundation.org.uk/
https://adhduk.co.uk/
http://www.addiss.co.uk/

See Also
Highly Sensitive Person (HSP) aka Sensory Processing Sensitivity (SPS)
Rejection Sensitive Dysphoria (RSD)

4

Autism

The learning from my research is that there is a wide range of types and levels of autism: the full spectrum, as it is known. In some cases, it is clear that a person is autistic, but for most, it is hidden. If you are asked to provide advice and support in an HR role, do not assume that you know anything about their condition. Have a chat with them, allowing plenty of time. Find out exactly what their needs are and what needs to be done to make the workplace more inclusive.

Mary's Experience

Our first interview was delayed because Mary had just got an ice cream out of the freezer. She explained that her 'executive function' was non-existent. The day before, she decided she needed a shower (something she is, in her own words, OCD about) moments before her support worker knocked on the door. The appointment was in her diary, but it didn't mean that she could make a decision about the order in which things should happen or whether there was sufficient time between appointments.

Having got her to start talking about life with autism, Mary was distracted by an alert on Instagram. When I got her attention, she explained that she takes scores of photos and videos of herself and uploads them to various social media sites. So much so that she gets blocked regularly and occasionally is banned. Why am I giving this detail? Simply because it will give you an idea about the complexity of autism.

Mary recognises that she can be impossible to live or work with. She suffers episodes, the most frightening of which make her hate herself and feel unworthy. She has refused most medications that have been offered on the grounds that their long-term side effects are still unknown; they do pacify her, and they make her drowsy and want to sleep, but they could damage her. Mary wants to be an engaged member of society, giving something back, so these side effects are unwelcome. She has accepted the help of support workers, and she was attending regular one-to-one therapy sessions until Covid-19 intervened.

Mary lives with a sense of paranoia. Her default position is to blame herself for anything that goes wrong. This means that even constructive criticism can be misconstrued and leads to a sleepless night or two as she tries to process the information. If she sends an email about something that affects her and doesn't get a response, she will often catastrophise the issue, jumping straight to the conclusion that the person no longer wants her in their circle, or worse, that she is about to be dismissed. The fact that she is aware of these issues, and can talk about them with me, doesn't mean that she can rationalise them in the moment or control them.

In the work environment, if something is of real interest to Mary, she can develop what she calls a 'micro-focus' on the subject and become highly productive. This has led to some excellent work, including research projects, art works, curated displays, exhibitions and shows.

Iza's Experience

Iza was formally diagnosed with autism at age forty-seven. It followed a series of disciplinary meetings where an alert HR Manager wanted to understand what the underlying issues were. Here was a person who was promoted to supervisor (after several years as an exemplary specialist cleaner) and had then failed.

Iza was referred to Occupational Health, and then on for a formal assessment with a psychiatrist. She explains that she was genuinely surprised, but that her parents and partner were not! Following the assessment, the company assigned extra support from another experienced supervisor and Iza learned how to deal with the new roles and responsibilities. She says that it was tough at first, and that she needed to learn things several times, but that her helper was tolerant and accommodating. Today she openly tells colleagues that she is diagnosed as autistic, what that means and how they can best work with her. Everyone has been very supportive and she is excelling in her role again.

HR Accommodations

Mary and Iza suggest the following:

- Be ready to double or treble the amount of time that you assign to the initial induction in HR. Whilst Iza had no issues, Mary needed to start to build a relationship beyond that which occurred at the interview and know that she has someone she can trust and turn to if things get difficult, without everything having to land in the lap of her line manager. In this way, she can keep a professional relationship with her boss and avoid it getting too close to her personal issues, which will flare up from time to time.
- If you elect to use an external occupational health service, ensure that one person is assigned to work with her. It is immensely unproductive for Mary to have to keep going through the process of relationship-building.
- Set clear expectations, and ensure that communications aren't ambiguous. If an email has been sent, follow up to check it has been understood in the way it was intended.
- Avoid surprises. A sudden call, text or email can cause concern and confusion, even paranoia.
- Autistic colleagues need extra time to process information. Like a chess Grand Master, they are processing every possible eventuality, including scenarios you could not possibly conceive.
- An autistic mind moves in mysterious ways and sometimes needs to be steered back to the question at hand.

- Have an appropriate support system in place. If Mary has a personal issue, she needs to know who she can turn to. If not dealt with properly, then she can go downhill, in terms of her productivity, relatively quickly. Given that she can get into quite difficult personal problems, her support person also needs a supervisor (in the confidential sense of a coaching supervisor, so that the burden can be shared). In Iza's case, the only support that she needs is her peer supervisor.
- Mental Health First Aiders should not assume they can step up to the mark. Their own training is not sufficient to help someone like Mary, and they may do more harm than good. Signposting is the best way forward.
- Think twice before reaching for the disciplinary code when someone like Mary misses an appointment. Remember that her executive function is nothing like that of others. She may have been distracted, a support worker may be helping her through an issue, or she might have got carried away in the moment, completing a piece of research and losing all track of time. If it is the latter reason, then be ready for something quite extraordinary to emerge.

Further Resources
https://www.autism.org.uk/
https://www.ambitiousaboutautism.org.uk/

5

Bipolar Disorder

As the name suggests, Bipolar refers to two states of mind (bi). People diagnosed have shown evidence to their assessor that they move between periods of mania to depression. For some, the swings are sudden, and they are far from hidden to the outside world. For others, they are disguised or hidden, sometimes by medicines or treatment, hence the inclusion in this book.

Mania is typified by a lengthy period of high productivity, sometimes sheer brilliance, where ideas and actions flow – often well beyond anything achieved by those who are not bipolar. But these episodes are balanced by periods of inactivity or depression, where the person gets angry or moody or turns in on themselves and goes very quiet. At its worst, the thoughts of a bipolar person can become suicidal.

When I first talk to Sheryl, she says that she always knew something wasn't quite right. From an early age, her behaviour was different to that of others, her energy levels weren't the same as her friends', and she struggled with her mental health. It all came to a head when she was sectioned under the Mental Health Act as clinically depressed. As part of her treatment for depression, she was provided with training in CBT (cognitive behavioural therapy) and counselling, but it wasn't until three years later that a consultant psychiatrist recognised her symptoms, ran a further diagnostic test and explained to her that she was bipolar.

At first, Sheryl was angry. Looking back, she recognises that she was in a 'hyper' phase, which she characterises as being when she is invincible. At these times, her tolerance levels drop dramatically; she speaks at high speed and isn't in control. Sheryl hates being hyper, and worse, she hates the issues it can create. On one occasion, she decided that the pipework for the radiators in a house she was staying in shouldn't be covered in paint, and so she spent all night meticulously stripping them down and then polishing them clean. Quite a surprise for the host! She explains that she exhibits all the traits of having OCD (obsessive-compulsive disorder); anything out of place is out of her control, and that makes her feel very uncomfortable.

One of the issues that Sheryl has to deal with is that she doesn't know when she is hyper; she has to rely on others to tell her. When she comes off the hyper state, she gets very tired and often crashes out. She will fall out with someone over something minor, say things that she doesn't mean and offend people without logical reason. Worst is when this leads to depression and her lack of ability to then do anything at all; even getting out of bed can be a huge issue. Sheryl says that her head feels heavy, everything seems heavy, and she just can't be bothered to do anything. People can speak to her, but she has no recollection of what they say. A fog descends over her.

To prevent these two states being hyper (or manic) one day and then down the next, Sheryl takes prescribed mood-modifying medicines that establish both a floor that she can't drop below and a ceiling that she can't climb above. As with many medicines, these have side effects. In her case, it is weight gain, something that she has to work at to keep under control.

The pandemic has stretched Sheryl to the limit, but she has been determined to stay on her medicines. She knows that she has too much to lose, including a good job, a car, a house, a new loving husband and the holidays abroad that she loves. Sheryl benefits from having one constant by her side, her son, who has a knack for keeping her grounded and appreciating life *with* the medicines.

HR Accommodations

Sheryl has some thoughts for making the work environment easier for people with bipolar disorder:

- Everyone has their own version of bipolar. Read about it and then chat to your colleague and find out how it affects them. Discuss what support they need and whether they want feedback if they appear to be manic or help when depressed.
- Bipolar people need structure, a set plan, objectives and to be made aware of those things expected of them. This is particularly important when starting a new role.
- Many lack confidence; take more time than usual to praise good work and steer them in the right direction. Avoid being patronising.
- Be prepared to forgive and forget if your colleague says something that hurts. Whereas most people will keep their thoughts to themselves, a bipolar person might express them out loud, albeit without the intention of causing offence. It is most likely a transitionary response and will soon disappear.
- Flexible working hours can be helpful, allowing more work to be done during hyper phases, but accepting that output might slow when depression kicks in (it still can play a part, even with medication). I heard about one example where annual hours are used to great effect in a research lab: the scientist will work for days and weekends at a time when verging on hyper, then disappear for a similar timescale whilst recovering.

Further Resources

https://www.bipolaruk.org/
https://www.mind.org.uk/information-support/types-of-mental-health-problems/bipolar-disorder/about-bipolar-disorder/
https://www.bipolarscotland.org.uk/
http://www.bipolar-foundation.org/

6

Blackouts and Hemiplegic Migraine

When Amina was in her early twenties, she had to abandon her law degree because she developed regular sudden blackouts. These would often result in injury as she would fall to the ground, hitting chairs and tables on the way down. As her symptoms worsened, she realised that she couldn't go out on her own, cross the road with safety, or do any of the other things that most people don't even think about. Her confidence was shattered. Initial basic investigations had been inconclusive, and no treatments were proving effective.

A while later, Amina experienced a blackout that resulted in a head injury, necessitating a hospital stay. Following further tests, a cardiologist found arrhythmia in her heart, which required an ablation (surgery to remove the tissue around the heart that is misfiring). The head injury had a further significant impact on Amina's life as she had lasting physical and cognitive symptoms that could not be treated. Thankfully Amina's symptoms from her head injury eventually resolved, partly because of her youth, and the ablation proved to have been successful.

But Amina wasn't out of the woods. Years later, she felt a pain in her face and at first thought that it might be a dental problem. It quickly became much worse, and one of her colleagues told her that she needed to seek help because she wasn't making sense when she talked on the phone. She called her GP, and by the time she phoned back, Amina had no idea of her name or anything about her circumstances. The GP called an ambulance, and the paramedics had to force entry into her house, taking her straight to the hospital. She was displaying many of the symptoms associated with a stroke, including paralysis and loss of feeling on her right side. Once there, and following more tests, it was discovered that she had a swelling on her brain as well as meningitis, and that when she had fallen, she had slipped a disc.

Amina was frightened, confused and felt she might be dying. The consultant diagnosed a hemiplegic migraine: a debilitating form of a chronic neurological condition that affects one side of the body. He provided immediate treatment for the infection and pain relief. Due to her sensitivity to light, Amina had to rest and sleep as much as possible in the dark.

During her stay in the hospital, Amina received an additional and unexpected diagnosis of syringomyelia, which is a rare condition where a syrinx, a fluid-filled cyst, forms within the spinal cord. The neurologist explained this might have been caused by her previous head injury or by meningitis. The condition can be progressive, with the risk of developing significant physical disability and other neurological symptoms. Amina was advised that a 'watch and wait' approach was the only option at this stage because there was a high level of risk with the extensive surgery that would be required. She now knows that looking after her spinal health and physical fitness are critical as she tries to avoid the condition worsening. This was a huge shock to Amina, and she is still coming to terms with her diagnosis. She feels a sense of a 'ticking time bomb' in her body, invisible to all.

The migraines persist, and whilst some medicines can help, there are still times when Amina needs to take time out and hide in a dark place to allow the symptoms to pass. She explained that she struggles with identifying as a person with a long-term condition, especially as it is not obvious to others. Working from home has significantly helped her and means that she can be more productive, but a flexible and empathetic manager has been the biggest godsend for her.

As Amina says, 'The key point for me in terms of management support has been that my manager has listened and sought to understand how these conditions affect me personally, rather than making assumptions, allowing flexibility when I have needed it. Particularly the 'whole person' approach, acknowledging how the physical illnesses have affected my mental wellbeing and continue to do so. She has been wonderful in helping me rebuild my confidence professionally and personally. I am very lucky; she is a fantastic role model.'

HR Accommodations
Specific adjustments that have helped Amina include:

- Phased return from long-term sickness after hospital treatment and surgery.
- Flexible working hours during migraines, avoiding the need for absence due to sickness.
- Homeworking when taking tramadol for pain relief, as driving is not possible when on this medication.
- Equipment: a supportive chair, sit/stand desk and wireless headset for voice/video calls.

Further Resources
https://www.migrainetrust.org/about-migraine/types-of-migraine/hemiplegic-migraine/
https://rarediseases.org/rare-diseases/hemiplegic-migraine/
https://rarediseases.org/rare-diseases/syringomyelia/
https://www.ninds.nih.gov/Disorders/Patient-Caregiver-Education/Fact-Sheets/Syringomyelia-Fact-Sheet

See Also
Migraines

7

Blindness and Vision Loss

But Ted, why is being blind a hidden disability? The answer is that it's not visible to everyone. I can illustrate this in two contrasting ways that have nothing to do with one's outward appearance. Firstly, one blind or poorly sighted person may not know that they are talking to another, and secondly, the pandemic has opened up all manner of new homeworking opportunities, and colleagues no longer necessarily come into contact face to face. A case in point for this would be Chioma, who was blinded in a car accident. She has been working from home as a sales rep for a company for three months, and her company still don't know that she is blind. She is one of the few who thinks that the pandemic has been a good thing! When interviewing or meeting with others using Teams, she wears dark glasses.

Her relatively recent breakthrough in finding a role belies the fact that Chioma lost her job from her previous employer (which involved a lot of driving), then spent a long time working through an insurance claim, and an even longer time in rehabilitation as she learned about her new unsighted world. Things that she had taken for granted were no longer as easy as they had been, or even possible. Chioma was, however, determined to succeed, and once she had her insurance money she invested in some high tech solutions to make her life as easy as possible. These included a high specification laptop, software and a camera that converts text to speech.

Prior to meeting Chioma, I interviewed Aidan, who has been blind since birth. What is it like being blind? Can we gain an insight? That's probably impossible. But let's give it a go.

When sighted people reference things like a large building (objects that are too large for him to touch), Aidan explains that he has the ability to conceive such concepts by continually learning and adding to his vocabulary, and understanding comparisons like small and large and wide versus narrow. He learned about shapes at primary school through tactile objects, and these help him to complete the 3D jigsaw puzzle in his mind.

The concept of colour is through learned understanding. He tells me that different colours evoke different responses, feelings and experiences in people, and he has learned to feel these for himself: red for excitement or anger, the calming nature of blue and the environmental credentials of green. By learning the differences that sighted people express about colours, he can get a feel for them and play a full part in conversations.

HR Accommodations

Chioma and Aidan suggest:

- A discussion with the IT team to provide a laptop with software that converts text to audio (maybe allowing the person to use their own familiar laptop if security can be resolved).
- Providing advance copies of presentation slides for audio conversion.
- A fixed (*not* hot) desk that they can get to know and make their own.
- Time with a colleague to learn routes to key places in the building (toilets, canteen, tea station, reception, lifts, etc).
- A tailored fire-evacuation plan.
- If the person has a guide dog, then discuss the needs of the dog and what additional measures are needed to support them (space to play, eat, drink and relieve themselves).

Some general tips from Aidan about being helpful as a sighted person include:

- Make sure the facilities team don't create new trip hazards without first alerting the blind person (like leaving a *This Floor is Wet* sign at the top of the stairs).
- Don't show a blind person a shortcut, as it will take them away from their known route and could leave them disorientated. Routes are carefully planned and part of their established routine.
- Don't make a big fuss in a social context. There's nothing more embarrassing than being announced to a room full of strangers when you just want to blend in.
- Be as discrete as you can when helping. This is not a moment for you to try and win an award for being a great citizen.
- When talking to a blind person, start by saying who you are. Just because they are blind or impaired doesn't mean that they can automatically recognise your voice straight off.
- Trim trees and bushes and take care of other objects that overhang walkways or pavements. Whilst a white stick helps find obstacles on the floor, it doesn't save heads from being hit by branches, signs and scaffolding.
- People with impaired vision or blindness have good and bad days. If you offer to help and get a gruff response, don't let it put you off offering help in the future.
- If you get in the way of someone with a white cane, don't scream or shout or make sudden or erratic movements. Stand still and allow them to go around you.
- If you see someone with a white cane walking very slowly, or moving in a circle, do approach them. The chances are they are out of their routine or are in a new area and need help. If you can get them to a landmark *of their choosing*, they can then re-orientate and get back on their way.

- Watch out for someone needing help on a day of extremes. Remember that a routine path can seem strange if the weather has taken away the temperature changes, the breeze or the sounds that a blind person is expecting and using for navigation. As an example, Aidan got 'lost' on his way to the restaurant because the fridge he turned right at had been switched off. The way the space around you works is different if you cannot rely on sight.

Regarding the offers of help that Aidan gets, he points out that the most important thing for him is to feel in control. If he has been consulted and then consented to walk with aid, knowing where he is going or which road he is crossing, then everything is fine.

Further Resources
https://www.rnib.org.uk/
https://www.guidedogs.org.uk/

See Also
Usher syndrome

8

Brain Injuries

Julie-Ann was in a rush. She had a meeting with her CEO, but before leaving home, she needed to tidy up to make things a bit easier for the cleaner. As she tried to put a bag on top of the wardrobe, a laptop slipped out and hit her on her head. She felt a bit stunned but jumped in the car. It was only a twenty-five-mile drive, but she had to pull over several times, as she was feeling dizzy and suffering from lapses in concentration. The effects of the concussion worsened, and, on seeking medical advice, she took time out to recover. But after six months, she was still suffering: Julie now had cognitive difficulties, she forgot things, she was getting regular migraines and suffering from sensitivity to light.

Whilst her GP had little knowledge about the effects of a brain injury and how to treat it, her occupational health team at work researched the issues and made a series of recommendations and adjustments to help her. A year later, still not quite feeling quite right, she pushed her GP and asked to be placed on the NHS brain injury pathway. Once admitted, she met a neuropsychologist and later, specialist occupational therapists that specialised in brain injuries. Learning different study techniques and mindfulness as per their recommendations had a significant impact on her symptoms and cognition.

In conversation, Julie-Ann explained that the most challenging thing was getting people to take her injury seriously. There were no visible outward signs, no walking stick or wheelchair, she could speak normally, but she would become overwhelmed by sound and light (especially in shops) and could no longer follow something as simple as a shopping list. She suggested that it's the human equivalent of losing 50% of your computer RAM (random access memory).

The best news came from a neuropsychologist that Julie-Ann met on her pathway. She said that her age was on her side and that she could retrain her brain. That ray of hope led to the pursuit of many exercises and ongoing treatment, meaning that Julie-Ann is now ninety-five per cent back to where she was before the incident. She controls her environment and tries to avoid situations that will spike her adrenaline or shock her eyes or ears.

HR Accommodations

Julie-Ann offers the following advice to HR teams (and parents, in case your child gets a bump on the head):

- Concussion and brain injury, however incurred, needs immediate rest and recuperation in a darkened and quiet area – even if the GP is saying that the injured person should remain active.
- Tinted glasses (or prescription lenses) help with bright office lights and computer screens.
- Consider home working for the injured person, where they can control the light and sound more effectively whilst in recovery.
- Don't rush them back to work; consider flexible work patterns and part-time working whilst recovering (and this can be many months).
- Seek support from occupational health, and take their advice on board.
- Ask IT to look at ways to reset a laptop and phone to cope with brightness or negative colours (white writing on a black background in emails).
- If working in an office, can the desk be placed away from strong light, glare and sound sources?
- Can a quiet space be made available, should a migraine attack occur or be imminent or for breaks?

- Offer support in finding and taking mindfulness lessons.

Further Resources
www.Headway.org.uk
https://www.thebraincharity.org.uk/

See Also
Aphasia
Hydrocephalus

9

Breakdown

The term 'nervous (or mental) breakdown' is not a clinical diagnosis. Instead, it is a phrase used to describe people who have got to the point where one too many things in their life conspire to create a period of immense emotional stress, which renders them incapable of carrying out their normal work, let alone their daily lives. Treatment and counselling nearly always help.

While a breakdown itself is unlikely to be hidden, the symptoms leading up to it may well be concealed. For many employers, it is still the case that mental health is a taboo subject, and worse, that when a case presents itself, the employer moves fast to find a reason to let them go. Erica was acutely aware of this. She was working for a small company with old-fashioned ideas about employee wellbeing, and she knew that she couldn't present a doctor's certificate to her employer that mentioned a mental health breakdown, a concept filled with embarrassment and shame.

Erica had felt that she was different for a while. She suffered symptoms of anxiety, a loss of focus and concentration, and was overthinking things. Insomnia had become her constant companion. At the start of her breakdown (which she can now rationalise retrospectively), she started experiencing hallucinations and wasn't able to hear when people were speaking to her. At the time, she didn't know what had happened or why she felt this way. She was scared, and felt increasingly isolated. She now recognises that trying to manage on her own and not seek help only made it worse.

Erica started drinking to ease the symptoms, but this led to deterioration in her overall health. There was no light at the end of the tunnel, and she knew she was losing control. She needed some space, and she needed to stop living a lie and pretending that all was fine, but she was too embarrassed to share her troubles with anyone.

Then it happened. Erica experienced a full breakdown. She woke up one day and felt that she couldn't carry on as she was. She couldn't stop crying. Fortunately, she was back at home at the time, and her mother gave her the confidence to go to see her GP. Unfortunately, the doctor's action was simply to prescribe medication and no other support.

After some months, her employer became concerned and asked her to see an occupational health doctor to make sure she was telling the truth and was actually sick. Erica was given access to a professional who was able to explain her condition, what was happening and what she could do to help herself. But Erica didn't feel she was able to face the shame of returning to work and needed to take action to change her lifestyle. She made the brave decision to resign and start afresh and return to education.

Later she met a trained counsellor, who explained what was happening, reviewed timescales for resolution, explained what to do when things got bad, and helped her regain control using tools like CBT, mindfulness and exercise. Erica has found these remedies simple yet powerful, and they have helped her turn her life around.

Erica's plea is straightforward: that HR teams do all they can to remove the stigma of mental health, to talk about it openly, to set up the right professional support, to provide easy-to-access counselling, allow flexible working including working from home as needed, but most of all to listen and work together to find appropriate solutions.

HR Accommodations

If someone is returning after a breakdown, try the following:

- Re-introduce them back into the workplace gently. Start with a chat outside of rush hour and progress in steps from part-time to full-time work.
- Listen and try to understand what the triggers might be. Avoid exposing the person to undue stress or anxiety in their first few months of re-entering the workplace.
- Provide flexible working hours.
- Create a network of Mental Health First Aiders and start getting people used to talking about mental health issues so that the stigma starts to reduce.

Further Resources

https://www.mind.org.uk/
https://www.mentalhealth.org.uk/our-work
https://www.turning-point.co.uk/

10

Breast Cancer

Claire had decided to take some time off work and explore the world. All her plans were going really well, right up to the point where she discovered a lump in her breast.

Skip forward two years, and Claire is now back at work and on a mission to raise awareness about cancer and how employers can help support their employees. She wants women to keep checking themselves and to talk to their doctor immediately if they find something untoward. Don't delay is the clear message: even if the health service is under strain, the earlier you get things dealt with, the better.

After finding the lump, Claire went through a series of tests, mammograms and scans. She waited two weeks for her appointment, then another week for the results. In her case, it confirmed her worst fears, and she entered a whole new world.

Surgery was up first to remove the tumour. Then chemotherapy to remove all chances of cancer spreading to other parts of the body. Finally, radiotherapy to kill off any rogue cells left in the area of the lump.

Claire says that the surgery was the easy bit, and after listening to the details of the subsequent chemo and radiotherapy, I can understand why. I'm going to go into the details here because cancer is a private journey, often hidden in the workplace for as long as possible by those that suffer. I believe HR people need to know and try to understand why their colleagues genuinely need considerable time off for treatments and recovery.

Chemotherapy

Everyone has their own experience with chemo, and there are many experimental medicines being used. A few ride through it without any obstacles, but the majority feel the side effects. Claire would attend the clinic and be fitted with a line, which would take the chemicals directly into her bloodstream, an act that in itself messed up her right arm. She describes the day after as feeling like she was on fire. She would be nauseous for a couple of days, reduced to an extent with another drug, and she would suffer from a poorly stomach for several days. She would feel lethargic and exhausted, and as if that wasn't enough, she started to develop other side effects after the first few weeks of treatment. In total, she received six rounds of chemotherapy which were three weeks apart.

Peripheral neuropathy, a type of nerve damage resulting from the treatment, meant that she couldn't feel the ends of her fingertips for about nine months. Her fingernails and toenails became brittle and blackened in places. She developed chemo-brain, which is like a feeling of fuzziness; she would struggle to find the right words and be forgetful. This lasted for about six months, and still rears its head now and then.

Claire read up on the subject and decided to try out cold capping to reduce the chances of hair loss and curl. This involves wearing a gel cap at -12C whilst undergoing the transfusion. The 'Paxman' cold cap, which made her look a bit like a jockey, froze the hair follicles, and it worked well, saving a good number of them. Once the chemo ended, her hair started growing back, fine like a baby's hair at first, but after a few cuts, it converted to chemo-curl hair (even more curly than before). Claire says that having an empathetic hairdresser was a lifesaver through this transition, as was a product that helped fill bald spots called Toppik.

Given that the world is now more aware than ever about viruses and bacteria, the other longer-term impact on her health was that the chemo meant that she was immuno-compromised. Claire had no defence against any disease, and even common colds would have a devastating impact as her body would fail to cope. The pandemic made this even more serious as Claire faced catching Covid-19. Thankfully, she was prioritised for the vaccination programme, but it leaves an additional lingering concern.

Radiotherapy

Claire underwent radiotherapy every day for two to three weeks, although obviously the prescribed therapy depends on the individual. She would travel to the regional centre, get changed and wait. The length of her appointment time was always variable because the nurses and technicians have to position the patient exactly before blasting the area with rays. The blast was quick, but the set-up typically took around twenty minutes. After getting changed, Claire would go home, always reliant on someone else since it's not sensible to drive during the course. Radiotherapy didn't make Claire tired, but it did cause painful burning to her skin, a bit like sunburn, which she soothed with E45 and aloe vera.

Today Claire lives with the after-effects from both chemo and radiotherapy, and every twelve months she goes through 'scanxiety', as she takes her next test and waits for the results. Is that phone call or letter going to be good or bad news? The results can entail weeks of waiting, and the anxiety builds every time.

HR Accommodations

As an HR Director, I have witnessed a range of reactions when someone receives the news that they have cancer. The most common is a stoic response, along the lines of 'This won't beat me. I'm going to carry on as normal.' This is either accompanied by a request that no one in the work environment is told, or the exact opposite that everyone is told and regularly updated. The former can be quite tricky. At some point, people in the team become curious about the amount of time off work the person is taking, why they 'aren't their normal selves', or similar questions that arise. You need an agreed plan to deal with this, and you will always need the line manager to be involved.

Throw out the sickness absence rules and work closely with the line manager and with payroll to make things as easy as possible for the affected person.

The following tips are drawn from Claire and others who have been impacted by cancer:

- A flexible approach to working is so important. In the initial stages, it may be that the person just needs sick leave and time to recover between each chemo or radio treatment, but when they start to return, remember that they may get tired quickly.
- Conversations are always best backed up with an email to confirm, to help counter the effects of chemo-brain. Cancer changes you on every conceivable level, and the treatment dulls you down. Chemo-brain can last for up to two years, causing forgetfulness, confusion and anxiety in the workplace. Be flexible and let them know they are still supported when they return to work.
- Counselling is an important resource to help overcome the trauma of the treatments and the realisation that all aspects of the employee's life will now be different. Beyond health matters, there will be ongoing impact on matters like life assurance, critical illness cover, driving and holidays, and other confidence-sapping side effects like early menopause, hair loss and lethargy. Find the resource through EAP, Occupational Health or elsewhere if it is not being provided by their doctor. Macmillan Cancer Support is great for such resources.
- Keep communication channels running, both officially from the company and through colleagues keeping in touch. Understand that responses may well be delayed, as the person is now living in a different chemo time zone. If you (HR) are going to be away, let them know who is providing cover. People being treated for cancer will have good days and bad days, so if they contact you with a query, be aware that it will probably be on a good day, and they may not be able to contact you on another day if treatment

is difficult for them. Be patient with them and give them plenty of time to respond.

- If you need to send any important information to the employee, for example, regarding changes to salary, do not do this just as you are leaving the office on a Thursday evening for a long weekend! The person may want clarification and someone to discuss it with. If you are not there to talk to, this will provide added stress.

- Finding cover for the work to be done, but without making the person anxious by replacing them with someone else, is a sensible way forward.

- If someone gives you an estimate of when you can expect them back at work, an estimate is all it is. Given the length of time that a programme of treatment is likely to take, extend all the same support that you would to a pregnant woman. Contact them a week before they are due to return and check in with them, extending sick pay arrangements as needed.

- Transitioning back to full-time employment after a long time away is difficult. It's actually much more difficult than leaving to go off sick. If your employee has had cancer, this might be the most traumatic thing they have ever dealt with in their lives, so be flexible with the amount of time they need on a phased return. Confidence will be low, and they may even be terrified that they can't come back and work at 100% capacity. Make the experience as easy as possible, with a briefing beforehand and flexible, part-time working building up to full time only when they are ready.

- As an HR person, stay in touch with the person's line manager after they return to work. There are no hard and fast rules for best practice when it comes to cancer. Everyone is different, but it would be useful for managers to have flexible guidelines to work with alongside their common sense and compassion. Ensure the manager is aware that the employee may not be at 100% working capacity so that they can quietly inform others not to come to your desk to demand you do some work for them in your first hour back in the office!

Further Resources
https://www.macmillan.org.uk/
https://www.mariecurie.org.uk/

See Also
Hodgkin Lymphoma
Prostate Cancer

11

Bullying and Mental Health

After building her career in human resources, Greta took time out to raise a family, returning later into a business partner role. She's not sure whether it was her lack of self-confidence or returning to work after a break that triggered what was to follow, but she is quite clear that she was bullied by one of the senior managers with whom she had to partner.

He was a tall, well-built and intimidating character who would lean back in his chair and watch her with a menacing expression. He had no interest in the management of his team, let alone being their leader. He demanded that Greta undertook all his one-to-one appraisals for him, saying that was her job, and asked her to sort out a competency matrix without offering any support, stating that he had read on the CIPD website that this was something HR people had to do. Charmingly, he told her that if the audit failed, it would be her fault and hers alone. He knew that she had to collect her kids from school and yet deliberately set meetings and interviews at those times in the afternoon to exert his control.

Greta explains that the odd thing was that she could advise others how to handle being bullied by him, but she couldn't solve her own case. Several times she broke down in front of her HR line manager and eventually was offered resilience training. Finally, Greta realised that her health was on the line. She wasn't sleeping well, she was getting snappy with her kids and her partner was feeling the strain.

Greta wrote everything down and then composed an email to her manager. The following day, Greta was invited to a project meeting with her line manager and the bully. She couldn't believe the insensitivity of her manager. She froze in the meeting; her heart was pounding, she couldn't concentrate and she couldn't speak. Her only thought at that moment was 'I hate you'. And that was directed at both her colleagues.

She left the meeting at the first opportunity, and to this day, has no idea how she got home. After the half-term break she returned and, now, in retrospect, realises she was behaving irrationally. If she saw the bully in the car park or walking along a corridor, she would hide from him. She was consumed with fear and hatred and realised that she had to resign. Even now, she freezes when she sees the same model car that he drove or his surname in another setting. It's moments like this that remind her she made the right decision.

One person's bully is, of course, another person's firm and decisive, action-orientated line manager. For many, admitting to being bullied is akin to admitting weakness, and in that way cases are so often hidden in the workplace. What we have to do is understand that when someone raises a concern, they won't have done it lightly. And if they present evidence, as Greta did, and they express their emotions and explain the impact that it is having on their physical and emotional health, then we have to act. This does not mean that we have to write a bullying policy and send it around. Most bullies do not realise that is what they are. They often believe that they are one of the few managers getting results and that others are far too lax in their style. Greta's manager should not have brushed her off in the first instance with resilience training. And she absolutely should have investigated her complaints when they were submitted in writing.

A claim of bullying is a grievance and needs to be treated with that level of seriousness. Someone independent of the main parties needs to be invited to talk to the parties and seek the views of others who might be impacted. Actions might include suspension if the allegations are substantiated. Sometimes coaching and training can help a bully see the problems they have created; in other situations, they need to either move divisions or even leave the organisation. Failure to do this can lead to serious complications, especially when people's mental health is being put on the line.

HR Accommodations
Greta suggests the following ideas to HR teams:

- Ensure that all line managers undertake awareness training in the understanding of bullying, its impact on productivity and how to support those who believe that they are being bullied. A statement of commitment to not tolerate bullying, made by the senior team, can really help with the messaging.
- Don't just publish a policy on bullying: make sure everyone knows about it and that there is a support network available for confidential advice.
- Ensure that any allegations of bullying are properly investigated and that those making the reports are properly heard. In some cases mediation will be required to find a solution. Follow up with retraining and support for all parties, and disciplinary action where needed.
- Provide appropriate counselling support from a third party for those affected.

Further Resources
https://www.bullying.co.uk/workplace-bullying-resources/
https://www.gov.uk/workplace-bullying-and-harassment
https://www.acas.org.uk/if-youre-treated-unfairly-at-work/being-bullied

12

Cerebral Palsy

Phoebe realised she was 'different' when she was eight years old. A new child arrived at her primary school, and instead of the child accepting Phoebe for who she was, the dynamics changed, and things became more difficult.

Cerebral Palsy (CP) affects all aspects of movement and coordination, as well as posture, tone, reflexes and balance. Sometimes it also affects speech, which can be slurred, and there may be issues with vision, hearing and swallowing. The severity of the condition varies from person to person, and no two people are affected in the same way. In Phoebe's case, both her arms and legs are impacted and she uses a wheelchair most of the time, with elbow crutches for moving around at home and in tighter spaces.

CP is thought to be caused by a change in the brain that is either present at birth or develops soon afterwards. There is no cure, although some treatments, such as physiotherapy, can help improve the impact of the condition, and some medicines are prescribed to treat side effects.

Phoebe was the only physically disabled student when she started at her primary school. Back then she was one amongst many young children, fully accepted by her peers. She was, therefore, disappointed when she was told that she would have to go to a different secondary school from all her friends. Thankfully there was an upside, as she was delighted with the extra support that she received in lessons.

Teenagers want independence, and for Phoebe, there were many restrictions to achieving this, and she ended up internalising her emotions around her difficulties in joining in her friends' activities.

During her teenage years, when Phoebe was occasionally feeling low, adults at her school would ask what was wrong. When she tried to explain, she received responses such as 'You're lucky you have a loving family', or 'At least you have a stable home'. It made her feel guilty and made her stop opening up, despite other adults at the school showing empathy.

It took until her early twenties to seek professional help when she recognised that her mental health was beginning to suffer. There is a learning for us all here, to think carefully before telling someone who has a condition or disability how lucky they are; sometimes, we just need to listen and hear those people.

Phoebe got her GCSEs, A levels and Level 2 and 3 in Counselling skills, all whilst volunteering in a school and working in Early Years. She's bright, easy to talk to and thinks deeply about a wide range of subjects. She loves football and has started to visit every stadium in the football leagues with her brothers, but she isn't perfect; she supports West Ham...

Having met Phoebe and been inspired by her, I am one hundred per cent convinced that she would add huge value to any organisation lucky enough to employ her. Making some accommodations to the work environment would be more than repaid by having the opportunity to benefit from her intellect, her ability, her sense of humour and her refusal to let anything stop her from achieving what she desires.

HR Accommodations

As a consequence of living with CP for her whole life, Phoebe has plenty of tips for HR teams employing or hosting someone with CP:

- Always ask them, listen to what they need and find the best solutions. Colleagues with CP are excellent problem solvers; they have spent their whole life working their way through a heap of issues and problems thrown at them!

- Please do not pity or feel sorry for your colleague, don't patronise them or speak slowly to them. Instead, treat them just like you would anyone else.
- If they are in a wheelchair, find an excuse to sit down and talk to them on the same level. Don't stand talking down to them any longer than is necessary.
- If they have a personal assistant with them (to move their wheelchair or open doors, for example), remember to speak directly to your colleague, *not* through their personal assistant.
- Sometimes speech may be slurred or slower than you are used to; give the person time. If you don't understand, just ask for the words to be repeated (better than misunderstanding by guessing).
- Speech can be impacted by illness or tiredness. Think about offering a morning interview to someone like Phoebe, and if they are working with you, offer to hold important meetings at the beginning of the day. For others, afternoons might be best; just ask.
- Think about access to the building, including doors and ramps. Whilst they're a requirement for new buildings and renovations, many older buildings are inadequate. Some main doors are on heavy springs because of fire regulations. Walk the routes, think about a wheelchair, how wide it is, and the angles needed to get round corners. Either put door openers on tricky doors or, at the very least, a bell to call for assistance.
- Consider kitchen areas: reaching for a kettle, getting into a fridge, the height of the light switches, coffee machines and fire alarms can all be problematic.
- Are photocopiers and other common use equipment easily accessible?
- Is the work desk (or interview table) suitable? What else might be needed? Are other areas such as meeting rooms appropriately equipped?

- Is there a disabled toilet facility suitable for a wheelchair?
- Is there a suitable fire evacuation plan in place?
- What do the first aiders need to know?
- What accommodations are needed to use IT equipment? If there is some special software that your colleague is used to, it may be more productive to continue with that rather than try to retrain them to fit the company standard.
- Some people with CP are unable to drive. Whilst the majority of trains and buses and a good number of taxis are modified, do think this through when arranging off-site meetings, parties and away days; you want everyone to feel included. For someone that does drive or who is brought to work by a friend, ensure there are adequate disabled parking or drop-off spaces.
- Taking a team photograph? Why not have the front row all seated? On your company website, use photos that occasionally include a wheelchair user.
- Be ready to be flexible in working patterns and times. It's not sensible to force someone with CP who is having a bad day to try to work; simply switch out to another day and move on. In fact, you might find your colleague is more productive if they can occasionally work from home. Just removing the need to commute can provide huge savings.
- Some people with CP have to attend regular hospital appointments. It is important to work with the colleague in relation to this, for example, allowing them to swap their days off.

Further Resources
https://www.cerebralpalsycymru.org/
https://www.scope.org.uk/advice-and-support/cerebral-palsy-for-young-people/

13

Chronic Fatigue Syndrome/ Myalgic Encephalomyelitis (CFS/ ME)

Chronic fatigue syndrome (CFS) is used interchangeably with myalgic encephalomyelitis (ME), and increasingly, people refer to the condition as CFS/ME. In Mikhail's case, he says that he is, literally, too tired to be bothered with what it is called. He just wants to find a way to cure it. He hates telling people that he has CFS/ME and then watching as a significant proportion metaphorically roll their eyes and ask him if he has tried any of the new sleep apps available on smartphones.

Mikhail explains that he is typically fast asleep when he is woken by his alarm and has often slept soundly for many hours, but he still feels exhausted. 'I feel like I have a constant low-level flu, just without the runny nose.' Furthermore, he is plagued by regular sore throats and headaches that aren't easily contained by simple analgesics. When he first presented these continuing symptoms to his GP pre-Covid, he was prescribed antibiotics to resolve the sore throat, but these only served to add a set of gastric problems to his symptoms. Other CFS/ME sufferers that Mikhail has met talk about muscle aches, feeling dizzy or sick and having sleep problems, but these are not symptoms that he has to contend with unless he drinks too much alcohol.

Following the failure of the antibiotics, his GP sent him for blood tests, and once the results were returned, he was diagnosed with probable CFS/ME only because the tests ruled out other conditions such as anaemia or an underactive thyroid gland. At the time of his 'probable' diagnosis, Mikhail was advised that there was no cure or current NICE guidance (the government body that recommends treatments for conditions), but that changes to his diet and lifestyle might help. Having read various websites, he decided to take a multivitamin tablet, but this has had no obvious benefit to date. Interestingly, he was advised against too much physical exercise, there being an ongoing debate about whether or not this might make matters worse.

Mikhail is well aware that he has a mild version of CFS/ME. He has met people who cannot work at all and live in a very limited world, struggling through each day and hoping that a cure will be found.

Mikhail's job is in the City of London, and he says that the saving grace is that he doesn't have to risk driving. He can sit back and let the train get him to Moorgate. This station has the advantage of being at the end of the line, so he doesn't have to worry about falling asleep, although going home, he has to set his phone alarm to make sure he doesn't miss his stop. Most days, he can perform his role reasonably well, but he believes that another promotion will never happen, having told his line manager about his affliction and been given a cold response. Mikhail has a generous holiday allowance and chooses to use it in small amounts at short notice. These are the days when he feels under the weather and needs a break. His boss has agreed to this as a way forward, but not once has he suggested that this should be treated as sick leave.

However, his employer has made one accommodation that Mikhail has found useful and links back to the advice given by his GP. Mikhail starts work about an hour before his colleagues and stays a bit later. This gives him the opportunity to take thirty-minute rest breaks in a designated quiet area that is also used by pregnant mums and others with conditions needing regular pauses. He finds these breaks helpful in managing his condition. His GP has warned him that if he doesn't pace himself, his condition could become a lot worse.

HR Accommodations

Having thought about the implications for others in the workforce, Mikhail recommends:

- When presented with an employee who has been diagnosed with CFS/ME, do not dismiss it. Diagnosis follows extensive tests and a lengthy wait, whilst doctors rule out other conditions. Once diagnosed, it means the person is affected by the condition and will need proper support and accommodations, not simply being told to get more sleep.
- Agree on a flexible work plan and utilise working from home where possible.
- Understand that sometimes your colleague will be so fatigued that any kind of work will be difficult. Find a way to allow sick pay systems to cope without triggering an automatic referral to occupational health every time. Consider annual hours as a possible solution.
- Provide a quiet area or rest room for breaks away from the noise of the workplace with comfortable, relaxing chairs.
- Encourage people to talk about their condition. This is one that is poorly understood, even by the medics, and needs to be taken seriously.
- Depending upon the diagnosis, the person may be registered as disabled and qualify for additional support. This is under review at present. Mikhail, for example, is not officially registered as disabled.

Further Resources

https://meassociation.org.uk/
https://www.meresearch.org.uk/
https://25megroup.org/
http://www.remembercfs.org.uk/

See Also
Long Covid

14

Chronic Obstructive Pulmonary Disease (COPD)

As with many people, COPD gradually crept up on Coraline. It started twelve years ago with regular coughing and phlegm. Breathlessness during exercise followed, accompanied by repeated chest infections and shortness of breath. The air sacs in Coraline's lungs are damaged (emphysema), and her airways are partially blocked. Her body produces more mucus than usual as it tries to clear the sacs and airways, in turn causing more coughing and wheezing. COPD can be considered a hidden condition because the severity and recurrence of symptoms vary.

Coraline is quite open about the reason why she has COPD. She was a smoker. She knows that her condition is self-inflicted. She explains that doctors and nurses can be quite dismissive for this very reason. Whilst smoking is the most common cause of COPD; there is a rare genetic disorder known as Alpha-1 Antitrypsin Deficiency (AATD), which includes COPD as one of its symptoms.

There is currently no cure, although in some rare cases the patient is offered a lung transplant to relieve suffering. Coraline is on Trimbow, which is the first three-in-one treatment for COPD. She also has a Ventolin inhaler for her breathing and is prescribed steroids to help reduce the inflammation during an exacerbation. She has been given a rescue pack by her GP, which includes antibiotics and steroids, should she have a really bad episode. When she goes abroad, she has to take this with her, along with her medical records. This means that she can look after herself at home without having to stay in a hospital, with the packs being replaced after use.

Coraline has to plan ahead and think through longer journeys, ensuring she builds in breaks to rest and recuperate before moving on. It limits her at times: she can't walk up the stairs with work colleagues (she usually needs to use the lift); she has to turn down some of the more energetic things that her friends invite her to (a day's shopping is just not possible); and housework has to be done in stages, with time to rest between chores. She says that when she pushes herself, she needs a long lie-down to recover from all the aches and pains that she suffers: it is 'all about breaking down tasks and pacing yourself'.

Coraline attends pulmonary care classes and takes part in Pilates lessons. She tries to manage her anxiety and stress levels (a trigger for an episode) and has learned when to say no. By keeping active and maintaining minimal stress, she finds that she can keep the condition at a steady state and not let it get any worse.

HR Accommodations
In the work environment, Coraline suggests:

- When your colleague first tells you about their condition, take time out to listen to them. If they have just recently been diagnosed, they may well be coming to terms with this life-changing condition. Try not to judge them for smoking (the likely cause); remember that many people are brought up in a family where smoking in the house was the norm.
- Where possible, offer a flexible working day. Many people with COPD and emphysema struggle at the start of the day and need to build up stamina. Interviews and important meetings are best held in the early afternoon, for example.
- Diary management is important. There need to be gaps between meetings where the person has to travel from one area to another, so that they can rest.

- At times of pandemic, help new colleagues understand that a COPD cough is not Covid and is a lifelong condition that comes and goes in intensity. Many COPD people will be asked to shield themselves until vaccinated; support them through this.

Further Resources
https://www.blf.org.uk/
https://www.copdfoundation.org/
https://naratbc.org.uk/copd/
https://www.emphysemafoundation.org/
https://foundation.chestnet.org/lung-health-a-z/emphysema/

15

Cystic Fibrosis (CF)

Cystic fibrosis can be considered a hidden condition because sufferers may appear healthy on the outside, while internally their organs are damaged. Cystic fibrosis is something that people are born with; it's a chronic genetic condition that is tested for in babies. Different people express their cystic fibrosis in different ways, but the common theme is that thick mucus builds up inside the body, affecting the lungs and the pancreas. In nearly all cases, it has to be treated regularly to prevent a build-up, which would be fatal if left unresolved.

In Nicola's case, her son George was born with CF, and she has learned how to help and support him. He requires two sessions of physiotherapy every day for a minimum of thirty minutes each. These exercises are designed to keep the airways clear and are followed by ten to fifteen minutes with a nebuliser. So that George can attend school, Nicola needs to get him up early in the mornings to go through the routine and be ready to go through it again in the evening. George needs enzyme supplements, depending upon which food stuffs he eats during the day, and he has to have additional A, D and E vitamin supplements because his body doesn't absorb them properly. He also carries a simple inhaler, should he need extra help with breathing during the day.

The good news for George is that science is developing fast. When he was born, his life expectancy was thirty-six years. With the arrival of new precision medicines, such as Orkambi and a combination therapy called Kaftrio, George's lung function will be markedly improved over time. Indeed, his life expectancy has already reached sixty, and he is just ten years old. Drugs are completely changing the landscape of CF care and will make the lives of CF patients so much easier in years to come. George used to have to take antibiotics every day, but with the new medicines, that is no longer necessary.

Ironically, George is envied by some of his friends. He has to maintain a high-calorie, high-salt and high-fat diet. He needs to eat three packets of crisps, or their equivalent, with his pills, as well as a full packed lunch. For him, regular eating and physio are actually more important than his education, although he hasn't missed out. Nicola says that he is mature before his time and has presented to his class on CF and its management. He doesn't yet have a regular cough, which will probably come later in his life, but he can be sensitive to temperature changes and is regularly having to attend clinics for check-ups and monitoring the effectiveness of new drugs.

The development of new medicines mean that many older CF patients must re-evaluate their lives. Whereas there was previously no need to save for a pension, that possibility now exists in more than their dreams.

HR Accommodations

There are more people in work with Cystic fibrosis than ever before, due to ongoing improvements in treatment and progressive accommodations that can be made to assist their employment. Nicola offers these thoughts for accommodations in the workplace:

- When someone tells you that they have CF, take time to understand what it means for them and the things that you can do to support them. Flexibility will be key, especially given the need to attend clinics for lung and liver function tests.
- If they require regular physio, you might need to make special allowances if travel is required in the role.
- A day's routine for someone with CF usually starts two hours or more before anyone else. That's the amount of time needed for

exercises, physio, nebulising and a high-calorie breakfast. Remember this when setting early morning meetings or when booking travel.

- Some people who have CF are exceptionally fit. Swimming is popular, as is the use of the gym. Keep up to date with how needs might change with the new drugs being introduced at the moment.
- During a pandemic having someone coughing regularly in an office can be off-putting. Agree to tell those nearby that it is CF-related and not contagious.
- Providing a parking space to reduce the distance to the desk can be helpful for those who are not so fit and able. Equally, working from home can lead to much higher levels of productivity.
- By all means involve Occupational Health when they are first recruited, but do not keep referring someone with CF to them for absence management issues.
- Your colleague may look fit and healthy as they put on a show to impress, but remember that their tiring schedule may take its toll.
- Some CF colleagues will suffer from bouts of depression or anxiety associated with concerns for their health. Provision of counselling support through Occupational Health or EAR can be helpful.
- Locate a desk for them in an area of the office that is free from draughts and cold air blowing through.
- If your colleague suffers from a prolonged or distressing coughing fit, help them find their inhaler and ask them if they want you to call a paramedic.

Further Resources
https://www.cysticfibrosis.org.uk/what-is-cystic-fibrosis
https://www.cysticfibrosis.org.uk/life-with-cystic-fibrosis/work
https://www.cff.org/

16

Death of a Young Child

Over ten years have passed since Charlotte lost her seventeen-month-old daughter, Lucie-Mai, yet she still flinches when people ask her how many children she has. Every January, her productivity nosedives at the anniversary of Lucie-Mai's passing, and the same happens when her birthday should have been celebrated. Each year Charlotte and her husband go away for a long weekend with her husband to remember their daughter. In Charlotte's own words, 'It's not something that you get over.'

In the work environment, Charlotte has learned that the best way to deal with this subject with new colleagues is to be up front with them. In this way, she avoids embarrassing them if it comes up in normal conversation, although she has to accept that some people don't remember and might still put their foot in it at some point.

Charlotte recalls that for the first three or four months after Lucie-Mai's death she suffered from insomnia. Returning to work after eight weeks of leave (her company were supportive), she would be wide awake at 3 am, responding to emails and working on projects, and then find herself crashing with exhaustion during normal working hours. She didn't want to take any extended time off work, she wanted the company of people around her, and thankfully her employer was willing to be flexible and give her the time she needed to start to recover.

Counselling worked well for her husband but not for her. Charlotte preferred talking to friends and colleagues, whilst her remaining children, aged six and eight at the time, were supported at school with counselling through play.

At a practical level, finances were tight, especially when both Charlotte and her husband were on sick pay. They found that the Civil Service Benevolent Fund could help with funeral costs and that the utility companies reduced their bills for a period of time. Not all these things are known by everyone, proving the point that it is worth asking around and seeing what is available.

Charities that specialise in supporting families with child loss include Reuben's Retreat, which provides short holidays for families who have lost a child or who are facing terminal illness with a child. Both professional and volunteer support are on hand as well as the chance to meet others facing similar problems.

HR Accommodations

Charlotte offers the following advice to HR teams about how best to work with someone who has just faced the death of a young child:

- Engage the person in a private conversation. Listen to them, find out what they need and express empathy. Provide a safe space and allow for silence – don't feel that you have to fill the void with conversation. Avoid saying that you 'understand what they are going through'. Unless this has happened to you, you will never know.
- Be generous with your compassionate, special or sick leave. Your kindness now will be repaid many times over in the future. And with the chance to recover properly before returning to work, you have a far greater chance that the person will return to higher levels of productivity sooner than if you force the pace, and they suffer setbacks. Charlotte explains that people who are forced back too fast are often those that suffer a full mental breakdown.
- Flexible working can be helpful. The chance to sleep in following a restless night and make up the hours another day can be enough

to make everything more tolerable. Working from home can also be beneficial.

- Signpost the person to useful resources, especially if things like funeral costs are playing on their mind. Given that they might not remember everything you say in the meeting because they are distracted, send an email to confirm and signpost links they need.
- Ask your Occupational Health team to provide support and talk to your MHFAs about bereavement, which all people face at some point in their working life, and how best to provide support, especially when a child has died.
- Ask the person if they would like you to tell their colleagues about what has happened. If they want to keep it confidential, then you should respect their wishes, but at a later point, help them to see the benefits of involving others, with understanding and support being key factors.
- Offer practical support in the work environment. Can you provide a private space to go when feeling low, or needing to make phone calls, or attend a Zoom counselling session? Offer the use of the photocopier and phones.
- In a larger organisation, consider the merits of employee passports: simple documents that people can take with them when changing line managers that explain their needs and accommodations.

Further Resources
https://www.childbereavementuk.org/
https://www.lullabytrust.org.uk/bereavement-support/
https://www.foryoubyyou.org.uk/
https://www.reubensretreat.org/
https://www.winstonswish.org/

See Also
Sudden Loss (Bereavement)

17

Depression

I count myself lucky not to live with depression, but I lose track of just how many friends and family members do live with it. Each has different symptoms, different episodes, different means of coping. The common link is that they can all appear to be relatively happy to the outside world, whilst inside they are fighting their own demons. And there is the issue, right there. Fighting demons is exhausting, especially when depression recurs regularly.

When I first worked with Ivana, I was impressed with just how many things she appeared capable of dealing with at once. Indeed, one of the team said she was the finest juggler they knew. Her role was to coordinate all the job role reviews for the company and run the annual performance-related pay review.

I remember going out with the team to play ten-pin bowling one Thursday evening after work. Ivana got several strikes and was second overall by the time we ended the game and went for pizza. She was chatting, laughing, discussing her plans for the weekend and interacting with the group. The next day she didn't arrive in the office at 11.30 am, with no prior communication. She sat at her desk and just stared at the window, leaving everyone feeling a little concerned. I was in a project meeting and received a text from one of the team leaders. I immediately left the meeting and tried to engage Ivana in conversation, with no success. I offered her help to put on her coat and got her agreement (a nod) to go for a walk in the local park.

At first, we just walked, saying nothing. Then she opened up with a comment about how cold it was. Bit by bit, she talked about her bouts of depression. She explained that they came from nowhere, without any warning, and could switch her mood 180 degrees in minutes. She wasn't aware of any triggers or solutions. She explained how she was made redundant from her previous role after a bout of depression had an impact on a big regrading programme that she was leading after a merger, and how she now feared for her job now that I knew about it.

After the weekend, I spent more time with Ivana, regularly going for a walk or a cup of coffee at a nearby café, which she would often leave untouched. I learned what depression was to her. She said that she was sad, helpless and felt worthless. She said that sometimes all she could see was her own shadow, which haunted her, and that it felt like she was wearing a heavy coat that was too big for her and weighed her down. And yet, there was hope. When offered the chance to go home early, she said that she preferred to stay; she wanted to pull herself out of it and knew that being alone at home wouldn't help.

A week after this bout of depression started, the medicines prescribed by her doctor began to take effect. This was rare, as most medicines in this field take many weeks to work. Ivana had held onto her pills for a few months, not wanting to use them because she and her partner were hoping to start a family. From what I could glean, her doctor had suggested that she restabilise herself before trying again in a few months' time. I was always impressed by Ivana's impeccable logic (necessary for her job) and the openness with which she shared quite personal details with me. She had been trained to use CBT techniques alongside her medicine, but was aware that CBT only worked for her if she was 'on the edge of depression rather than deep inside it'.

Ivana's love of logic sometimes made things worse. She always wanted to know exactly why her mood had changed and what the triggers had been. She analysed herself in such detail that she had trouble getting to sleep. I remember one conversation where I was unable to get a word in edgeways as she walked through the issues that she felt had triggered an episode and how she could learn from it, and then she proceeded to beat herself up for allowing it to happen. Looking in from the outside reminded me how lucky I was.

With the medicines working their magic, Ivana's ability to interact with others improved rapidly, and her productivity mushroomed.

Recently I caught up with her, and I have a lovely update that might give hope to some. Ivana gave birth to twins after I had left (about three years after the episode mentioned above). When she fell pregnant, she went through a rough patch, feeling sick, questioning whether she had done the right thing, and worrying endlessly about the possibility of post-natal depression. The exact opposite occurred! She has not been depressed since giving birth. In true Ivana fashion, she has read numerous articles about it and believes that the hormone shock that her body went through in childbirth has somehow reset her chemical imbalance and left her without any side effects. She even joked that she had refused her partner a third child on the basis that it might reset to the wrong balance again!

HR Accommodations

The advice Ivana would give to line managers and HR teams looking after someone diagnosed with depression is as follows:

- Those who are diagnosed are in a better place than those who have not been diagnosed. If you see someone with any of the many symptoms of depression, be there for them and encourage them to seek professional help.
- When someone presents with depression, listen to how it affects them and then build a support framework around their needs. This will be different for everyone, as everyone is impacted in a different way.
- Ivana recommends that everyone has a buddy, someone in the office who watches out for them. With line managers operating across sites in different time zones, the reality is that they can't

keep an eye on everyone. A buddy can ask how someone is and then keep following up until a proper discussion is held and the matter moved towards resolution.

- Don't tell someone who is depressed to 'snap out of it', to 'try to smile', or 'to get a grip; it's not as if you're disabled'. And don't tolerate others saying such things. If anything, they just make matters worse. As Ivana says, it's not as if they want to be in this state. Instead, be empathetic, offer support and signpost them towards professional help.
- Encourage the person to lead as healthy a lifestyle as possible. One of Ivana's line managers went for fast walks with her at lunchtimes, which she thinks helped her keep fit and less likely to become depressed.
- Understand that an inability to concentrate on work or complete tasks might be related to depression (itself linked to poor sleep and/or poor nutrition). Mention you have noticed this and give them a chance to open up and talk about it.
- Offer flexible working where you can. The person may need some space now but could well be fine at a later stage.

Further Resources
https://www.mind.org.uk/
https://depressionuk.org/

18

Diabetes, Type 1

In Type 1 diabetes, the body's immune system attacks its own pancreatic beta cells. These are the cells that produce insulin which, in turn, controls blood glucose levels. It is why it is sometimes called 'insulin-dependent diabetes'. Without the insulin regulating the blood, sugar levels can run sky high and cause damage to internal organs, ultimately resulting in coma or death. Once diagnosed, patients must monitor their blood sugar level and then administer sufficient insulin to bring their bodies back into balance. Significantly, they also have to ensure that their blood sugar level doesn't drop too low. If it does, they can become hypoglycaemic (often shortened to 'hypo'), a condition where the lack of blood sugar leads to shaking or sweating and sometimes confusion and the inability to concentrate. A person with Type 1 diabetes looks no different to anyone else, which is why it can be considered a hidden condition.

A common misconception is that people need injections when they start having a Type 1 hypo episode, largely because it has been popularised on TV shows. What they actually need is to raise their blood sugar levels. Another misconception is that Type 1 diabetics can't have anything with sugar in it; they can! They can eat or drink whatever they like, so long as they administer enough insulin to counterbalance the number of carbs, so please don't exclude them from regular birthday cakes or chocolates.

Type 1 (10% of people have this type) is quite different to the more common Type 2 (90%), which is prevalent in overweight and/or older people. In Type 2, the body continues to create insulin, but the bodies' cells refuse to react to it. Type 2 is usually brought about as a result of poor diet and lack of exercise, and is normally controlled by diet, exercise and medicines.

Stephanie's Experience

Stephanie was diagnosed with Type 1 diabetes at age fourteen when her mum realised that she was drinking and peeing more often than usual and that her sleep patterns were more irregular than you would expect with a teenager. Blood tests confirmed her suspicion, and Stephanie was admitted to the hospital to get her diabetes under control.

Stephanie explains that it is a fine balance to control sugar levels manually. This involves continually monitoring blood glucose levels and administering the correct dosage of insulin to maintain a stable level, which is usually agreed with a health care specialist and tends to be between 5 and 7 mmol. If the levels drop too low, usually as a result of having too much insulin or missing a snack, Stephanie will start to feel shaky and may get a headache, begin sweating or even assume a drunken appearance. Sometimes this can happen very fast and lead to her feeling faint and having to find somewhere to sit or lie down quickly. Stephanie knows at this point that she has to boost her sugar levels as soon as possible. She carries jelly babies and apple juice with her, which quickly bring glucose into the bloodstream. In addition to these hypo treatments, Stephanie also has GlucaGen (a fast-acting prescribed treatment), which can be used with assistance from someone else if the hypoglycaemia has become too severe for her to treat herself.

The opposite of a hypo is if blood glucose levels are running too high. Symptoms of this can be extreme thirst, frequent peeing, nausea and feeling lethargic. Untreated high blood glucose levels (hyperglycaemia) can cause dangerous levels of ketones in the body and serious damage to internal organs. Hyperglycaemia can be treated by increasing exercise levels or by taking insulin.

Whilst there are various forms of medication for Type 1 Diabetes, Stephanie's treatment involves injecting fast-acting insulin prior to each main meal and once a day injecting long-acting insulin. For Stephanie, the quantity depends on the number of carbohydrates in the meal and her blood glucose levels at the time. Based on these numbers, she calculates the dosage of insulin to maintain a stable blood glucose level. The calculation is usually one unit of insulin for every 10g of carbs, plus any correction dosage that may be needed if the levels are running higher than they should be.

Lisa's Experience

Lisa was ten years old and had been ill for a few weeks. Her weight had dramatically reduced to the point where her clothes were falling off her, she was drinking lots of sugary drinks and was urinating more than usual. The GP ordered blood tests, and the results were so poor that she was admitted straight to the hospital.

Lisa doesn't remember much about the next few days, but she was administered insulin until her body responded, and she was held in the hospital for so long that she had to attend the hospital school. She was taught how to inject herself and learned that only she could look after herself. Her body was producing no insulin; if she didn't take this seriously, she could die – not an easy fact for a ten-year-old to digest. She returned to her normal school on a part-time basis as a changed person and had to adjust to her new life: weighing foods, calculating the carbohydrates and injecting insulin in the right quantities.

Today Lisa carries a kit bag with essential supplies wherever she goes, and she has an insulin pump that automatically supplies her body with a baseline quantity of insulin. She then adds extra by dialling up the pump ahead of mealtimes and will sometimes reduce the flow if exercising. The pump is sensitive to bumps, and risks like being jostled on the tube mean that she has to find a private place to reset it.

Lisa's blood sugar levels can be affected by stress, illness and pain. Her job is to keep the blood sugar levels at a happy level throughout the day. She is helped by the use of a disc monitor, about the size of a 10p coin, which is attached to her upper arm. This gives a constant read-out on her smartphone.

Every so often, Lisa is still caught out by a drop, or excessive increase, in her glucose levels. She carries a medical alert card that she hands to the paramedics on such occasions. It explains her condition and what actions they should take if she faints or falls into a sleep from which they can't wake her. Thankfully, it is used very rarely these days.

Lisa explains that, given her compromised immune system, she is susceptible to every bug and virus that goes around the office. A common cold for a day or two for most people can last a week for her. During the pandemic, she was asked to be extra vigilant, albeit not to shield, something that many diabetics found somewhat controversial.

Complications that come with being a Type 1 diabetic include changes to eyesight, nerve and kidney damage, circulation problems and heart disease. Lisa currently has a diabetic-related swollen tendon condition that has already required one surgery.

HR Accommodations

Stephanie and Lisa make the following suggestions for the workplace:

- When someone tells you that they are Type 1 diabetic, have a chat with them to understand how they are managing the condition. Ask them what to do if a sudden hypo comes without warning and what signs to look out for. Agree that it is okay to tell them if you think they look like they might be close to an episode.
- Agree to let co-workers know about their condition, also first aiders and security staff (where late working is involved) on site. Ensure first aiders know how to deal with a severe hypo (e.g. how to use GlucaGen if kept at work).
- Allow flexibility in working hours for clinic visits and for additional time off for recovery if they have an episode.

- If the person has to self-inject before meals, provide a nicer place to do this than the toilets if possible.
- Allow for additional time off if the person is either trying for a baby or becomes pregnant. A woman with Type 1 diabetes will be invited to more clinics than usual.
- There may need to be restrictions in place for driving or the use of machinery; if in doubt, refer to an occupational health specialist.
- Ensure there is an accessible fridge for the storage of medication. Some types of insulin must be kept cold or they will become ineffective.
- Type 1 diabetes is an auto-immune condition, and employers should appreciate that sufferers are more susceptible to picking up bugs. Your colleague may need extra time off for bacterial infections and viruses.
- Understand that some diabetics need to eat sweets or drink glucose drinks during meetings when their monitor alerts them; they are not being disrespectful. Equally, they may need to either dial-up their insulin or self-inject before a meal.
- Remember that it is exhausting to be a diabetic, so show empathy and understanding, and allow flexibility in work schedules. Consider home working where possible.
- If your colleague looks a bit drunk, do not begin disciplinary proceedings: help them sit down. If conscious, they will know what to do once reminded. If not, or if they've lost all sense of what is happening, call an ambulance.

Further Resources
https://www.diabetes.co.uk/
https://www.diabetes.org.uk/
https://jdrf.org.uk/
https://www.drwf.org.uk/about-us/who-we-are

19

Dyslexia

When she was young, Danielle simply thought that she was poor at spelling compared to her friends. It wasn't until she was twenty-seven years old that her dyslexia diagnosis lifted that huge weight from her shoulders. In retrospect, she's a bit annoyed. If she had known about it during her school days, she feels she would have been able to do even more; instead, she felt her hidden condition held her back and made some part of education more difficult. She sums it up by explaining the day she was diagnosed was the day she finally learned she was not lazy or stupid.

Dyslexia affects 10% of the population, is a lifelong condition, and, when formally diagnosed, is recognised as a disability in UK employment law. When a dyslexic person tries to read a page of writing, they see letters floating on the page, and words and letters getting mixed up, a bit like trying to read using someone else's strong prescription glasses after a few too many glasses of wine.

For many years Danielle hid her dyslexia, working extra hours to keep on top of her workload. But recently, she has become comfortable with telling people. By talking openly about it with colleagues, she can be much more productive, and she has found everyone is supportive. When it comes to problem-solving, she is super-human; it's when she has to write it down that things are slowed up. Her colleagues have learned that she is at her best when she is involved in a debate or project team that is talking through an issue, with someone else taking notes, rather than everything having to be submitted into the likes of Slack or Trello.

Danielle explains that she can prepare reports quickly, but they are then error-strewn and need a fair amount of time to edit. That editing needs to be done by the use of software because she can't 'see' most of the mistakes. She values her paid subscription to Grammarly, which helps a bit, but even that app suffers from some of her first attempts! For important documents, she will ask a colleague to give a final review before publication.

Danielle believes that she probably has mild dyscalculia (numbers rather than words) as well as some short-term memory loss that is often associated with people who are dyslexic. Working on spreadsheets and transposing numbers can, therefore, be quite an issue for her.

Some dyslexic people also struggle with maps and directions, albeit this has been mostly resolved in recent years by the use of mobile phone apps with audio direction, such as Waze and Google Maps.

HR Accommodations

In terms of accommodations at work, Danielle suggests the following:

- Flexible working really helps, as does an acceptance that extra time needs to be allocated for some tasks which require reading or writing.
- Pay for a subscription to a service like Grammarly, which helps correct common errors and build confidence. Note that this is US-based software, which occasionally provides some interesting results of its own.
- Ask the IT team to set up a dyslexic-friendly font (one which has been shown to be easier to read by people with dyslexia), the best background screen colour (e.g. Word doesn't have to be black on white) and an anti-glare filter.
- Provide text to speech software.

- When presenting, talk through key items on slide decks and don't assume that they are easy to read. Give the person the opportunity to talk through their own materials as they may be able to articulate details they can't easily convey via written materials.
- Ask the training team to switch away from e-learning and back to verbal or team-based learning.
- Have a ream or two of cream paper available, or whichever colour the person finds best. Printing on coloured paper often helps, as the contrast is reduced.
- Consider using voicemail rather than texting to leave a message.
- Educate the team on dyslexia and how to be supportive.
- Where possible, provide a private space for work that requires concentration or allow the person to work from home when they have to write up a project or read something ahead of a meeting.
- Don't ask your dyslexic colleague to take minutes of a meeting.

Further Research
https://www.bdadyslexia.org.uk/
https://opendyslexic.org/

20

Ehlers-Danlos Syndromes (EDS)

The Ehlers-Danlos syndromes (EDS) are a group of rare genetic conditions affecting connective tissue. EDS affects just one in five thousand people. Connective tissue is found throughout the body, providing support and holding structures in place; however, with EDS, a genetic mutation causes the tissue to be stretchy and fragile. It's an invisible disability and is difficult to diagnose; it can take a decade or longer for diagnosis.

Natalie had a difficult and long journey to diagnosis: eighteen years. She injured her knee when she was eighteen years old and, following surgery, she began to experience pain in her hips, back, neck and jaw, as well as fatigue, dizzy spells and digestive problems. Many doctors and consultants tried to treat these individual symptoms. Each time they would look specifically at one body part and ignore the fact that there were multiple issues occurring that could be connected. Few GPs view their patients in a holistic way, which to be fair is not easy when they are only allocated a short time slot for each consultation.

During examinations, doctors frequently commented on Natalie's hypermobility and asked her to perform various 'party tricks', but dismissed this as unrelated to her pain. Over the years, she was given various diagnoses ranging from Chronic Pain Syndrome to Reflex Sympathetic Dystrophy, Osteoarthritis, Fibromyalgia and more.

Ten years after her knee injury, Natalie encountered a work colleague with similar symptoms. She had been diagnosed with EDS and was convinced Natalie had the same condition. After some research, Natalie began to suspect that her symptoms were indeed indicative of EDS and decided to ask her GP for a referral. When she saw her GP, she was told, 'EDS is incredibly rare, and you couldn't possibly have it.' The insinuation was that it wasn't a 'physical' issue.

Natalie left the appointment without a referral, feeling disheartened and undermined. Another GP told her to accept her deteriorating health would mean she would never work full-time, and she would have to live a life with physical limitations. For a twenty-something, that was a brutal message to hear.

For decades medical students have been taught that 'When you hear hoofbeats behind you, don't expect to see a zebra'. This means, don't look for the surprising diagnosis – look for the obvious, usual and common one. The zebra has been adopted as the symbol for people with EDS as, 'Sometimes when you hear hoofbeats, it really is a zebra'. Zebras are recognisable by their stripes, but no two zebras are identical. This is a fine metaphor for EDS; the condition can affect people in different ways, and for some, it can be relatively mild, while for others, debilitating.

Roll on another five years. Natalie decided to re-investigate the issues with her health and sought private treatment. She was fortunate to be in a financial position to afford this. Luckily, one of the consultants who was examining her knee was himself hypermobile and referred Natalie to one of the top rheumatologists with a specialism in EDS. He diagnosed her with hypermobile Ehlers-Danlos Syndrome or hEDS (previously known as EDS Type III), the most common of the thirteen types. Natalie says this was a revelation. The doctor took a full history and finally connected all of the dots. He explained that EDS is genetic, so it's present from birth. Suddenly, there was a clear explanation for her childhood issues with sprained ankles and wrists, the dental overcrowding and why local anaesthetic had little effect, plus why she'd experienced back and sleep issues as a teenager. Her consultant now started to review appropriate treatment therapies, no longer simply sending her home with painkillers.

Natalie's joints and skin are 'lax and stretchy', meaning that it's easy for dislocations, subluxations (incomplete or partial dislocations) and bruising to occur. Pain then follows as the muscles and nerves are stretched beyond their comfort zones. She explains that she bruises easily, so it can be quite a sight for the uninitiated. To help prevent dislocating joints, Natalie may intermittently use a splint, brace or support, depending on the area affected. For example, she wears leg braces at times and will use crutches when her knee joint has been frequently subluxing or 'giving way'.

Commuting to work can be problematic, and, as a consequence, she can be much more productive when working from home. It is Natalie's experience that passengers don't stand for healthy-looking people on packed trains, even if you are wearing a 'Please offer me a seat' badge or using crutches. Sitting still for long periods is also challenging as she needs to move regularly to prevent the overuse of muscles and joints from becoming locked. Managing the condition requires resilience. There are difficult days, and flare-ups do occur, but she successfully works full-time, is married and has two small children.

Working from home enables Natalie to be more productive, as she's able to manage her condition better. For example, when you're in the office, there are unspoken social conventions that can make it hard to change your position/posture, it can be perceived as fidgeting, or if you need to stand part-way through a meeting when everyone is seated, it raises eyebrows and questions, so you tend not to do so. Beyond avoiding the commute, which can be fraught with stressful physical challenges, working from home facilitates changing positions/posture, taking a regular stretch break (without having to leave your desk for fear of odd stares), control of your desk set-up (so you don't have to worry about your desk being readjusted by a hot-desking colleague) and general options to make yourself more comfortable (such as using support cushions or ice packs/hot-water bottles).

Aside from the physical challenges of EDS, the years it can take to get a diagnosis can take a psychological toll. For Natalie, after eighteen years of being dismissed, belittled, undermined, doubted and disregarded, finally having a diagnosis felt like vindication. Having your physical symptoms and pain ignored while having your mental health questioned is draining. It can also lead to a medical version of imposter syndrome; you begin to doubt yourself: 'Are my symptoms that bad?', 'If they can't find anything wrong, maybe there's nothing to find?' Receiving the diagnosis of a genetic condition is difficult, but conversely, it can feel cathartic; once you know what the condition is, you can address it at long last.

At first, Natalie was nervous about disclosing her condition to her colleagues. Even when she began telling people about it, there were moments where it was easier to downplay the challenges. For example, on one occasion, after just receiving her sit/stand desk (in an office where they were a rarity), a colleague she barely knew walked over and quite aggressively asked, 'Why are you special?'. Thrown by their approach and not wanting to explain the complexity of having hEDS, Natalie simply replied, 'I have back problems'. The colleague's response was to roll their eyes and walk away. This interaction made Natalie feel nervous about using her desk; it dredged up feelings of imposter syndrome, and she began to question if her condition 'justified' her having the desk. A trusted colleague who had witnessed the interaction took her aside, and her kind words made Natalie realise that she shouldn't let the jealousy of others impact her health. Since then, she has been more open about her condition. It can be uncomfortable at times, as people can be insensitive and even hostile as they are biased towards what 'qualifies' as a disability, but she feels like the only way to change these perceptions is to advocate for herself and others.

Trying to understand the impact of something like EDS is difficult. Natalie referred me to Spoon Theory. It's well worth looking this up if you are unaware about it. In essence, everything she does, every day of the year, uses up both physical and mental energy. Natalie only has a limited number of energy units to use before she is exhausted, or worse, becomes vulnerable to another symptom rearing its head. She has to make choices. Choose one thing, and that denies another. People with EDS are not limited by the hours in the day but by the physical and mental energy units at their disposal. This doesn't mean that a person with EDS is less capable of performing at work. Many people with the condition are exceptional high performers adept at juggling demanding roles and the complex needs of their condition; however, a supportive environment makes a significant difference in aiding them to maximise productivity.

HR Accommodations

Natalie has some tips for HR teams and line managers to make life a bit easier:

- Read up about EDS and try to understand it. Chat to the person and be led by them; everyone's experience and symptoms are different. EDS often has comorbidities (meaning one or more conditions can be present at the same time) such as Postural Tachycardia Syndrome (PoTS), gut dysmotility, chronic fatigue, Cranio-Cervical Instability (CCI), Mast Cell Activation Syndrome (MCAS) and more.
- Encourage the person to come to you if their needs change. Remember that connective tissue is found throughout the body, so symptoms can change by the day, and something that isn't an issue today, could be tomorrow or in a month or a year, so you may need to check in regularly.
- Discuss flexible working and allow working from home, which can lead to much higher levels of productivity. Provide the appropriate equipment to replicate the work set-up at home.
- Conduct proper workstation assessments. Don't just use the standard DSE assessment. Talk about the adjustments needed and make sure the person has a dedicated desk, not a hot desk. This may seem like a trivial issue to some, but remember, each

time the person with EDS has to readjust their workstation, they are using valuable energy that could be better spent elsewhere.

- Provide a sit/stand desk both at work and at home, if working from home is an option. This will enable the person to adjust their posture and reduce the problems of knees, feet or hips locking, as well providing a supportive and easily adjustable chair with height-appropriate footrest.
- Ask IT to provide different mice (for example, a vertical mouse) and keyboards (for example, a shorter or ergonomic keyboard). Consider voice-activated software for people who struggle with the joints in their hands, wrists and arms.
- If the person has issues with regulating their body temperature (one of many autonomic nervous system symptoms that people can experience), support them with options such as having an additional heater or fan to use.
- Avoid asking your colleague to use busy public transport; being forced to either sit or stand in the same place for long periods can lead to big issues.
- If you're arranging a conference or an away day, consult with your EDS colleague about possible problems. Add in lots of extra stretch and movement breaks.
- Don't assume that an EDS colleague is bored or uninterested when they appear to be fidgeting in a meeting; they might just need to readjust their joints.
- When organising interviews or meetings, remember that stairs could be problematic.
- If you have on-site parking, enable the person to use a space near their office.
- Brain fog and fatigue can set in during the afternoon and evening, so before arranging interviews or key meetings, check with the person regarding the optimal time for them.

- Provide a place to stretch and exercise (maybe a prayer room or a first aid room) or offer the person the use of a small meeting room.

Further Resources

https://www.ehlers-danlos.org/

https://www.ehlers-danlos.com/affiliates-support-groups-and-charities/

https://butyoudontlooksick.com/articles/written-by-christine/the-spoon-theory/

See Also

Hyper Mobility Spectrum Disorder

21

Endometriosis

By its very nature, endometriosis is often left undiagnosed for many years as GPs initially try to treat the underlying symptoms by supplying painkillers, hormonal contraception and advising on diet and lifestyle. With this condition the female body grows extra womb lining tissue in other areas of the body: often on the ovaries, fallopian tubes or elsewhere within the pelvic cavity, even spreading to the bone. This tissue behaves in the same way as the womb's lining and bleeds during menstruation. However, it cannot shed in the same way as the lining of the womb due to its location and therefore causes significant pain, inflammation and scarring, sometimes even adhesions between the pelvic organs. In some cases the growths on the ovaries are called endometrial cysts, or endometrioma. Symptoms of these conditions include fatigue, intermittent and heavy menstrual bleeding, spotting, digestive problems and pelvic pain during sex or going to the toilet.

While endometriosis is a hidden condition, it is widespread, with one in ten women affected by it on a four-stage clinical scale: I-minimal, II-mild, III-moderate, and IV-severe. Research has shown that pain levels do not correlate to the stage of the condition. Currently, a diagnosis of endometriosis can only be confirmed following an expert MRI scan or following investigative surgery by a gynaecological specialist. Treatment options range from painkillers and the use of hormones to removal of surplus tissue or cysts by surgery, depending on how invasive the additional growth has become. Even surgery is not always curative, with symptoms returning over time.

If left untreated, endometriosis can lead to either infertility or difficulties conceiving, both of which can carry a heavy psychological cost.

Kaya's Experience

When Kaya was finally diagnosed, she had to deal with several competing emotions. Relief that she knew what was happening inside her body and that a treatment pathway had been created, but also a loss of confidence and realisation that her life would forever be different. Some patients lose the chance to have children. Others find that conception is much more difficult. These concerns play tricks on the mind and can lead to mental health issues.

Kaya recommends that, as employers, we need to encourage people suffering from chronic recurrent pain to see their doctors and press for referrals until a diagnosis is made. We shouldn't assume that someone regularly complaining of sickness or backache is trying it on – they may well have an undiagnosed condition. Sometimes antidepressants and painkillers have a role to play, but often they can mask something that needs to be diagnosed and properly treated.

Whilst surgery for endometriosis should be recorded as sick leave, your colleague will need active support through the subsequent period of adjustment and any mental health side effects that accompany the change. Hormonal treatments can lead to mood changes, body temperature and tiredness, all of which require empathy and tolerance rather than warnings and monitoring.

To help ease the pain, Kaya is prescribed Tramadol, and she also uses a TENS machine. On those days when her condition flares up, she either needs to take time out to rest and recover or sometimes can work from home, but driving to work is not an option. A flexible approach from her manager works well.

Jess's Experience

Today is not a great day for Jess. She is in pain and feeling nauseous, which means that every so often she needs to take just ten minutes to go to the bathroom, throw up, have a breather, drink some water and then get back to the job in hand.

Jess was only formally diagnosed with endometriosis (or endo as she and many others call it) recently, having lived with its symptoms for years and having even suggested to her doctor that she might have it. The sorry story goes back to age fourteen and an emergency appendectomy. Every so often, Jess needs to have surgery to remove internal surgical scar tissue from the appendectomy, and at her last appointment her surgeon finally admitted he had found the tell-tale signs of endometriosis.

Jess has an unusually high pain threshold compared with other patients, which is probably a part of the reason why she had endured the effects of endo for so many years without letting it get the better of her. Her current consultant wants to avoid additional surgery to remove the tissue simply because of the number of times that she has had to have surgery in the past. Instead, he is trying a hormonal injection called Prostap, which induces menopause by reducing oestrogen production in the pituitary gland, giving the endo tissue nothing to feed off. This leaves the condition dormant until the effects of the injection wear off and oestrogen production restarts. If this works well and the side effects of Prostap are manageable, it may be a way to control the endo. The extra good news is that this chemical procedure is reversible and does not interact with the medication Jess takes to control her epilepsy. There is no cure for endometriosis; however, the symptoms can be managed, and this is the best way that Jess has found to do this. She cannot stay on Prostap forever, but it is working well for now.

Mona's Experience

Mona has probably lived with endometriosis for most of her adult life, albeit she was unaware until a routine pregnancy scan picked up the tell-tale signs. She has had to go to hospital on several occasions to have cysts of significant size (8-10 cm) removed from her ovaries, as well as surgery to remove endometrial tissue that caused one of her fallopian tubes to stick to the wall of her womb. Each round of surgery has required time away from work for the operation and for subsequent rest and recuperation.

What makes Mona's case different to that of Jess and Kaya is that she has only ever felt pain just before the time when surgery became critical, and she has never suffered from bleeding. She believes that the endometriosis affected her ability to conceive her first child and is pleased that it was diagnosed, because the knowledge that her fertility was reduced meant she could plan for siblings sooner rather than waiting until it was too late. As with many hidden conditions, this again shows how different people's experiences of the same condition can be.

HR Accommodations

Jess and Kaya say that their accommodation needs for endo are relatively simple in the work environment. On challenging days, it is sensible to take more breaks than usual or work from home if possible. Aside from that, flexible time off for hospital appointments and for days when the pain is at its highest level is invaluable. For Mona, her needs were for care and support when surgery was required, and for cover during her convalescence.

- When someone tells you they have endometriosis, listen to how it affects them and find a solution tailored to them. Read about the condition so that you understand it. Remember that it is likely to be present for most of their working life.
- Flexible working and working from home when needed are the best accommodations.
- If flex working is not possible, then a review of sickness absence policies is vital to reduce the number of times an endo patient has to be reviewed for days off.

Further Resources
https://endometriosis-uk.org/

https://www.endofound.org/

See Also
Fibroids

22

Epilepsy

Jimena was fifteen when she was diagnosed with epilepsy. She woke up in the hospital and was told that she had been spasming on the floor and had passed out, which was termed a 'grand mal' seizure (sometimes also called a tonic-clonic seizure). She felt drained, nauseous and exhausted. She was unable to remember anything that had happened that day or even that week or where she was when she had the seizure – gaps in her memory had to be filled in by her mum and the school friends who had witnessed it. She underwent tests and scans over the following month to determine her diagnosis. Over the next few years, she was given six different medicines to try and control her symptoms, but none of them worked.

Jimena has spent years developing her knowledge and educating others on exactly how her epilepsy is triggered. She knows that, unlike the stereotype, her seizures are not triggered by flashing lights: hers are triggered by stress and overtiredness. Jimena has a chemical imbalance in her brain, and any stress leads to neurons in her brain misfiring. The electrical activity literally knocks her unconscious and causes full-body spasms, causing damage to her brain and body. Due to the amount and intensity of the seizures she has experienced, Jimena says she has suffered more bumps, bruises and broken bones than the most hardened stunt actor!

Growing up, the constant seizures and trips to the hospital meant that Jimena struggled to complete her qualifications. Her school was concentrating on their most able students and trying to move up the league tables. The staff there failed to recognise that Jimena had so much potential, and she was left behind due to her condition. Finally, at age twenty, she was asked to try levetiracetam (marketed as Keppra) and success! The drug is believed to work by inhibiting presynaptic calcium channels, which reduce the release of neurotransmitters and therefore dampen the electrical storm associated with a grand mal seizure.

Jimena has learned to recognise when a grand mal is going to happen. She suffers around twenty minutes of petit mal seizures before the grand mal occurs. She takes these warning signs, also known as an aura, seriously and immediately finds a safe space to lie down until it is over. The petit mal stuns her with a sharp pain in her head, which can leave her unconscious for a second or two. Once the grand mal has occurred, Jimena is violently sick and needs around twenty-four hours of bedrest to recover. After that, she is back up and running, much more quickly than the old seizures, which could take her out of action for several days at a time.

Jimena has experienced many line managers in her years of working. Most have been understanding of her condition, some not so good. She is lucky right now to have a manager who has given her carte blanche to use the spare space in the office when she needs somewhere safe to lie down. She will also tell her if she appears to be becoming a bit distant and distracted, another early warning sign.

HR Accommodations
Jimena's thoughts about the work environment for an epileptic are:

- It is essential to tell a new manager of your diagnosis and explain. If you do not do this, they will not understand how to help you, which could be detrimental to your health.
- When someone discloses that they have epilepsy, talk to them about how it affects them, as it is different for everyone. Ask them what happens during a seizure, what should be done and what

the after-effects are likely to be. Educate yourself about the condition and learn to recognise the signs of a seizure.

- Ask for permission to tell the first aiders and immediate work colleagues and the security team (especially for out of hours work).
- Obtain emergency contact phone numbers. Jimena has her phone permanently unlocked with her mum's number on speed dial, so she can come and pick her up and take her home or to A&E, depending upon her condition.
- Seizures can affect people's memories, especially short term. Offer to help get them back up to speed and remember what they were prioritising as soon as they are back at work.
- Some of the epilepsy medications have side effects. In the case of Keppra, anger or even rage can flare up (thankfully not for Jimena) – be ready to be forgiving and understanding.
- Allow for flexible work schedules. Your colleague will not want to keep taking sick days; they might even feel guilty. Instead, it might be best to allow them to make up lost time when they are ready and to take days off at short notice when they need to.

Further Resources
https://www.epilepsy.org.uk/
https://epilepsysociety.org.uk/

23

Fibroids

Benedicta was initially brought up in Togo and Ghana, where the cultural norm is that if you have to suffer, you should suffer in silence. So that is what Benedicta did. From puberty onwards, she suffered heavy periods and irregular bleeding but told no one. She says that the pain was excruciating, and sometimes all she could do was curl up with a hot water bottle for days at a time until it passed. After arriving in the UK, she mentioned it to her GP, and following some tests and scans, she was told that she had fibroids, which explained the pain and flow.

Fibroids are small growths of fibrous or muscular tissue that develop in or around the womb. Even though they are also called uterine myomas or leiomyomas, the good news is that they are not cancerous. Aside from heavy and irregular periods, they can cause abdominal and lower back pain, a need to urinate often, mood swings, anaemia (due to loss of blood) and constipation.

Four types of fibroid have been identified: intramural fibroids grow inside the muscle layer of the uterus; subserosal grow from the uterus into the pelvic cavity; submucosal develop from the inner lining of the uterus towards the uterine cavity; and pedunculated are attached to the uterus by a narrow stalk. Many fibroids are only the size of a grain of rice, but they can swell to the size of a grapefruit if left untreated.

Fibroids can be controlled by the use of a range of different medicines, depending upon their size and location and to some extent by diet. Sometimes they are removed by surgery, the most dramatic of which is hysterectomy, which itself necessitates a significant period of recuperation. Benedicta was invited to try out a technology that has been developed in the last decade: a procedure called uterine fibroid embolisation, where the blood vessels that feed the fibroids are blocked so that the growths die and fall away.

And the good news? Well, Benedicta has lived with this condition for many years. It is now under control; it did not impact her ability to have a beautiful, healthy daughter; and she has her faith to guide her.

HR Accommodations
Benedicta has the following suggestions for the workplace:

- Although it might not be easy to talk about, it is important to understand which symptoms the woman suffers from and then make accommodations based on that. Listen carefully, read up and find out about the treatments or possible surgical interventions that she needs to undertake and with what regularity they occur.
- Find a flexible way to work with her. When a heavy period requires visits to the toilet every hour, then working from home is the most sensible choice, and sometimes sick leave is essential, but her absence doesn't need to be reviewed just because the recording system says so.
- Where surgery is required then all normal steps around support need to be put into place. A full hysterectomy requires a significant period of recuperation (eight to twelve weeks is common), and can be followed by a further period of adjustment as hormones settle. Menopause is often triggered in such circumstances. Support that is sometimes overlooked by doctors is for the mental health of someone who goes through a change as big as this.
- Make allowances for mood swings; show empathy when she is short with you. She might be experienced regular stabbing pains,

and something that you consider important is less significant to her at this time.

Further Resources
https://www.fibroid.network/
http://www.britishfibroidtrust.org.uk/
https://www.uhs.nhs.uk/OurServices/Radiology-scansandimaging/PatientInformation/FibroidEmbolisation.aspx

See Also
Endometriosis
Menopause

24

Fibromyalgia

This is a hidden condition that affects almost seven times as many women as it does men. As such, it is often brushed aside by line managers in the same way that myalgic encephalomyelitis (ME) is. Also known as FMS (fibromyalgia syndrome), symptoms include heightened sensitivity to pain, 'fibro-fog' (memory loss and lack of concentration), muscle stiffness, tiredness, difficulty sleeping, migraines or headaches and sometimes irritable bowel. It's not known why people develop fibromyalgia, but the medics have found a major stress event in life, such as an injury, operation, giving birth or death of a close relative may trigger symptoms. Lady Gaga has talked openly about her experiences, which has given hope to many.

For many people, fibromyalgia is accompanied by one or more other conditions, such as arthritis and carpel tunnel syndrome, which can confuse an early diagnosis. Even when a patient is diagnosed with this condition, there is no current cure. There are a number of approaches that can help, which include cognitive behavioural therapy (CBT), antidepressants, painkillers and changes in lifestyle.

Freja talked to me about her experiences. She started to develop symptoms when she was eighteen, but it wasn't until a decade later that she was diagnosed with fibromyalgia, and that was after the horrific experience of being run over on a road crossing.

Prior to the diagnosis, Freja struggled to get line managers to understand her needs, even though they were great people. With the diagnosis, a weight has been lifted, and she can now explain what her condition is and how it is best resolved.

After diagnosis, Freja took the antidepressants that were prescribed, but after a short while she rejected them due to their side effects. One of Freja's loves in life is going to live rock gigs (when I boasted about having seen Led Zeppelin in their heyday, Freja boasted about AC/DC and going to a Kiss concert in full make-up), and she realised that she just couldn't enjoy a live performance whilst taking medicine. Her senses were dulled, and she didn't experience the euphoria that going to a live gig normally provided. She has now made her own adjustments; she takes the seated option wherever it's available and knows to book the following day as a holiday to recover!

Freja gets what she calls 'brain freeze'. When this occurs, she can be perceived by others as being either lazy or not listening. A coping mechanism that she deploys is to wear headphones and listen to music so that she can concentrate and keep on track with her work.

When we were talking about resources (listed below), Freja made the point that some groups can lead you into depression or even despair. She cited a Facebook group in which people seemed to try and outdo each other with the severity of their symptoms, belittling those with a milder condition.

Freja is well organised. She has kept a record of her symptoms and all her medical appointments since age twenty. This has been invaluable when talking to specialists or a new locum GP at her own surgery. Initially, she was denied an opportunity to visit a migraine specialist, and she was told that her condition was caused by being a control freak. Thankfully she now has a great GP, who is both understanding and helpful in supporting her as she manages her condition. It is essential to ensure that she attends the appointments that she needs to build into her life, but also that she allows for rest periods after undertaking activities that can be quite exhausting.

HR Accommodations

For Freja, the things that help her and should be considered by employers wishing to be supportive include:

- Flexible working: there are times when Freja simply needs to rest and recuperate. If given time off, she will more than make up for it later that day or another day.
- A quiet space: a quiet room or space to go to when a migraine attack occurs is essential, with a supply of cold water.
- Handrails: helpful where there are slopes or steps.
- Hyperbaric oxygen therapy: not normally available on the NHS, but occasional sessions can make a huge difference to her mobility and brainpower.
- Freja can't hold a phone easily for anything more than a short period, so her IT department have supplied her with headphones as well as an ergonomic keyboard and mouse.
- Lighting: the areas she works in (and at home) have dimmer switches to suit her needs.
- Communal facilities: small details are important and need to be remembered. For example, someone changed the coffee jars at work, and Freja couldn't open them.
- Line manager: Freja is blessed by having an amazing line manager, whom she has nominated for an award. She says that being open, explaining the condition and its symptoms have led to a wonderful supportive relationship.
- Diversity and Inclusion champions: when set up in the workplace, they give people the opportunity to seek advice and support without having to be reliant just on their line manager or HR.

Further Resources

http://www.fmauk.org/
https://migrainetrust.org

25

Foetal Alcohol Spectrum Disorder (FASD)

Although much less well known and rarely discussed, FASD is probably as prevalent as autism and ADHD. Like autism, everyone is affected differently by it, and there are many levels of impact on people's lives, from limited to severe. As the name suggests, FASD is a series of conditions that are caused by a pregnant woman drinking alcohol. The alcohol passes directly from the mother's bloodstream into the baby, at the same levels, and can cause damage to the foetus in many different ways, both physical and mental. There appears to be a correlation between the amount consumed and the severity of reported cases, and in 2016 the UK's Chief Medical Officer advised that 'no alcohol be consumed in pregnancy and when planning a pregnancy'.

In 2016 Svetlana Popova and colleagues published an article in *The Lancet* which discussed comorbidity (a link) of FASD patients with other conditions: 50% had ADHD, 62% had vision impairment, 58% suffered hearing problems, 83% experienced speech and language delays and 91% suffered from impulsivity and inappropriate behaviour. Most children and adults diagnosed with FASD have a normal IQ but a spiky behavioural profile. They blow hot and cold, act on impulse and often struggle with a lower working memory than most, meaning a complex set of tasks with multiple steps may prove impossible unless written down and followed carefully.

Hajra was diagnosed with FASD as an adult after a psychiatrist reviewed her early life and current issues and rejected the GP's belief that she might be autistic. Hajra gave me some examples of how FASD affects her. She explains that when she was working in a busy restaurant, she would go and clear the table but then forget to clean it and put out the new cutlery. She would forget a word; it simply wasn't in her brain. When questioned about this by her supervisor, she panicked and failed to see a way to resolve the problem. Looking back, it was obvious, but not at that point until she was told point-blank.

Hajra has suffered several annual appraisals where she has been asked to try to be more of a team player and not rely on others to cover her mistakes, but she isn't aware that she has made them, and this makes work life difficult. During our interview, Hajra went off track on several occasions when answering a question and then failed to respond to my cues to get back to the matter at hand. I can imagine that if I was her supervisor, I would struggle to keep my patience after a while.

In her social interactions, Hajra confides that she often fails to recognise other people's positive intentions, takes things too literally and often snaps. As a consequence, she has only a few close friends, most of whom are lifelong.

HR Accommodations

For Hajra, accommodations in the workplace might include:

- Greater tolerance of behaviour that is out of the norm, understanding that the person may not be aware of the hurt they are causing. Having signals or time outs to review problems when they occur.
- Flexibility to work when the person is at their most productive. Possible use of annualised hours rather than fixed.

Joanna Buckard, Specialist Projects Co-ordinator at The National Organisation for FASD, has written the following excellent factsheet for employers (their website is a great resource):

FASD and employment

All people with FASD are different and will therefore have varying needs. People with FASD often have many wonderful qualities, such as being outgoing and friendly. People with FASD are often determined and want to work hard and please those around them. Like everyone else, people with FASD have different skills and talents; common areas of excellence include being artistic or musical, working with animals and children and computer skills.

Employers should undertake FASD training to understand more about the condition and to support the understanding that FASD difficulties are not intentional but a recognised part of their neurodevelopmental disorder and to be supportive and flexible.

It is important to ask the individual how FASD affects them and what strategies work for them. It may help some people with FASD to bring materials with them to such a meeting to aid their memory or to bring a support person. It is important to consider that they may feel frustrated by the impact FASD has on them. They may additionally be managing fatigue as well as anxiety and poor self-esteem. People with FASD may benefit from having the same shift pattern rather than changes, especially ones with short notice. Some people with FASD may benefit from a 'Buddy' system so they have somebody to go to whilst working who may be able to offer prompts such as with transitions during the day like break time.

Once a person with FASD has mastered what was expected in their job role, it is prudent not to expect that they can necessarily add to this. It may lead to the person becoming overwhelmed and less able to function.

Communication

People with FASD are often friendly and sociable and can express themselves well. However, their understanding of spoken or written language may be lower than it seems. They may take literally what has been said. People with FASD may struggle to pick up on non-verbal cues from others. Unwritten rules, including ones around shared areas such as the kitchen, may not be obvious to someone with FASD. What can help?

Staff training on FASD to promote awareness and inclusivity.

Use simple, clear and concrete language. Use visual aids.

Unwritten rules are made concrete by using a sign in clear, accessible language and, where possible, with an accompanying picture.

Have a communication book where work to be done each day is broken down into step-by-step instructions, and any priorities are clear and concrete.

Video instructions and being able to record meetings to allow for rechecking what was said.

Induction and training

People with FASD learn differently and, due to difficulties with processing information and memory, may benefit from a longer induction/ training process and that the tasks are demonstrated rather than described, with a written version to refer back to. Job shadowing. A visual map of the work environment can be useful.

Weekly support meetings

Discussion about what is coming up that week and a written step-by-step plan help to prevent surprises.

Working environment

Having a fixed desk where the person can have things kept in the same place would benefit somebody with FASD. The stress of finding a desk or not knowing where things are can heighten stress and anxiety and affect productivity.

People with FASD may get overwhelmed by sensory experiences such as uniform, bright lighting and noisy environments. Allowing flexibility over the uniform, aids such as earphones and sensory breaks can help.

Breakout room

Having a quiet area when a person with FASD can go to when they are overwhelmed is crucial so that they can regulate before returning to their task.

Memory

As memory can be affected, people with FASD may benefit from memory aids such as job sheets, picture aids, verbal prompts (one at a time).

Executive functioning

Executive functioning skills can be affected, including starting a task and sequencing, which affects linking previous and new tasks, changing from one task to another task and being easily distracted. It can be difficult to plan and organise tasks, keep track of time and control impulsivity.

Applications

Voice recognition software such as Dragon.
Brain in hand app to aid executive function.
Grammarly.'

For others, it will depend entirely upon the symptoms that they exhibit. By its very nature, FASD has hundreds of physical manifestations, which can range from vision to hearing, digestion to mobility and comprehension to cognitive ability. Listening to and understanding the needs of your colleague is an important first step to helping make the workplace more inclusive for them.

Further Resources

https://nationalfasd.org.uk/
https://canfasd.ca/wp-content/uploads/2018/09/Guide-and-Final-Report-Supporting-Employment-Success-in-FASD.pdf
http://fasdunited.org/
https://www.nofasd.org.au/

26

Gender Dysphoria and Reassignment

Discomfort with the gender assigned at birth is often felt in early childhood. In the past, it was called 'gender identity disorder' or 'gender incongruence' and sometimes 'transsexualism'. Around puberty, the discomfort and feelings either intensify and become much more difficult for the person to live with, or change – sometimes reverting to the gender assigned at birth, sometimes a conscious decision to be non-binary. In the UK at sixteen, you can apply for a name change by deed poll, and at eighteen, you can obtain a gender recognition certificate (GRC). The importance of the GRC is that you can then change your birth certificate and marry with your confirmed gender.

In Jayne's case, she was about four years old when she realised she wasn't comfortable being labelled as a boy, and she was thrilled a couple of years later when a shop assistant referred to her as a girl when she was shopping with her mother. She says that her childhood was strange: the world was telling her she was a boy and that she needed to look in the aisles with boys' toys and clothes, but she was always more attracted by the girls' aisles and grew to hate her assigned male name.

When Jayne reached eighteen, the current options weren't available, and so she went to college and then into work as a male research scientist. At around this time, she joined the church. She chose a conservative church, and reflecting back now, thinks it might have been a form of self-loathing. She saw quite a few members of the LGBTQ+ community joining, maybe thinking that if they prayed hard enough that their thoughts will go away, and they would become part of the 'normal' population again.

After twenty-six years as a scientist, Jayne felt the calling to the ministry and studied theology at college before being ordained. She had to put all her thoughts about gender to one side and play out the male minister role in full, winning over the hearts of her parishioners with her gentle and compassionate approach to life.

Living a lie takes its toll, and Jayne became depressed. She was in a male body, pretending to be a male minister. She arrived at a dark place, recognised it, and made the decision that she had to accept who she was. She confided in a few of her friends whom she knew were gay. They understood, kept her confidence and gave her the strength to slowly tell more people. Eventually, she told the whole congregation about her identity during a sermon. By that point, she was accepted for who she was by the majority (indeed, by that time, most of them already knew). There were a few outliers, people who insisted on calling her by her male-assigned name, but everyone else adapted over time. Jayne resigned and decided to move on and set up a new life as a minister with a new congregation in a new area.

Whilst applying for a change of name by deed poll is a relatively well-established process (albeit painful when you consider that employers, utilities, councils, banks, GP, DBS, driving licence and passports offices must all be told), a gender change is much more problematic. Getting a gender recognition certificate requires that you attend two clinics with a registered specialist practitioner. Where Jayne lives, the current waiting list to simply get the first appointment under the NHS is four years, followed by another four years' wait for the second appointment! And all this has to be resolved before you can even consider hormonal treatments or surgery to go through the next stages of gender change. Jayne comments that you also need to be well enough off to pay for the private track to get your certificate or take a risk and buy the drugs on the black market.

To achieve physical change, testosterone acts quickly when a female wishes to develop a huskier voice and grow facial hair, whilst for a male to transform is a longer and trickier path, which often involves surgery. Trans men undergo 'top surgery' (removal of the breasts), whilst trans women undergo 'bottom surgery' (removal of the penis and testicles, and creation of a vagina).

HR Accommodations

Jayne has been quite open about her transition and received some publicity about her case, probably because of the link with her church. She has some thoughts about how an employer can make the work environment more welcome, and therefore more inclusive, for someone thinking about coming out with gender transition:

- A policy statement on the website, and mentioned in recruitment advertising, sends a strong message that you support people who have reassigned their gender or are considering it. By doing so, you will open up your organisation to a greater talent stream.
- Helping form LGBTQ+ networks and finding allies takes a policy statement to the next level. Role models are even more effective should they wish to be open about themselves.
- When someone talks to you, be led by them in the speed with which others learn about their transition. Some people will want to tell everyone themselves; others will seek help with messages to team members.
- Take practical steps. The next time your washrooms are being refurbished (if not before), consider making them all gender-neutral with cubicles and some private make-up rooms.
- Make name changes easy for people (this applies to simple marriage name changes as well!). Have a co-ordinated IT/Payroll/HR/Telephony/Security one-stop-shop in place.
- Allow time off for clinic appointments, and be as flexible as you can in the initial weeks; this can be an emotional period. If a part-

ner is involved, there may be a divorce or break-up to resolve as well. Support your colleague now, and you will be remembered for years to come.

- Consider how pronouns are used at work. Some organisations are introducing the option on intranets and email to include things like 'he/him' and all variants after the name.

Further Resources
http://www.gendertrust.org.uk/
https://www.beaumontsociety.org.uk/
https://gic.nhs.uk/info-support/support-groups-and-resources/
www.gires.org.uk/
www.genderedintelligence.co.uk/
www.gendergp.co.uk/
www.mermaids.org.uk/
www.genderkit.org.uk/
https://www.gov.uk/apply-gender-recognition-certificate
https://www.gov.uk/change-name-deed-poll/make-an-adult-deed-poll

27

Hearing Loss, Profound

To really try and understand the issues faced by someone with profound hearing loss, I was privileged to be able to interview Iona. Whilst most of the interviews for the book were carried out over Zoom, we agreed from the start that this would not be easy. Iona explained that it takes a while to learn to lip-read another person well; the current voice to type software is in its infancy (anyone who has watched news bulletins auto-transcribed will know just how poor these can be), and a face-to-face meeting was ruled out by Covid. Instead, we opted to write back and forth until we were both happy with this chapter. Most of the following content comes from Iona, who is far more accomplished writer than I am (a hint for your next career, Iona!).

People with profound hearing loss are often referred to in common parlance as being 'deaf', but that word conjures up an image of sign language users rather than the rich mix of different conditions and accommodations that people make. 'Hard of hearing' suggests that making things a bit louder or wearing hearing aids resolves the problem, which isn't the case. Hence profound hearing loss is a better descriptor.

Iona was formally diagnosed with profound bilateral sensorineural hearing loss as a young child after her mother realised she wasn't responding to many sounds. 'Profound' is the highest level of hearing loss, above 'mild', 'moderate' and 'severe' on the clinical scale, whilst 'bilateral' means both ears. Her loss occurs in the inner ear and the quietest sound she can detect is around 90 decibels (think of a lawnmower or motorbike). High-pitched frequencies can't be picked up, however loud they are, meaning that there is only a narrow range that she can hear.

Iona feels vibrations, especially the bass vibrations, at clubs and concerts. The way that she knows the dishwasher cycle is complete is by feeling the machine for vibrations, given that she doesn't pick up the alert tone emitted by it, for example.

When she wears hearing aids, she can pick up some lower-level frequencies, but the sound isn't clear. Given that her condition is hidden, the main benefits of wearing them are that they provide a visual clue to others that she has hearing loss, and it provides a welcome distraction from the tinnitus that is ever-present (akin to the ringing that you get in your ears after a loud bang or attending a loud gig, but it doesn't go away).

To quote directly from Iona: 'I am very upfront with people about my hearing loss. I explain that although I wear hearing aids, they only pick up a small range of sound, and I am heavily dependent on lip-reading. I also say that if I don't respond, I'm not ignoring them – I'm just not aware they are speaking to me. I ask them to get my attention before they start to speak, ensure I can see their mouth and not stand in front of a window or other light source (this casts a shadow on the face). It also helps if the topic is made as clear as possible at the start of the conversation, as this helps to fill in the blanks with lip-reading. The person should speak at their normal pace, be prepared to repeat things if asked and also be conscious that accents and facial hair can have an impact on lip-reading.

'Some people are uncomfortable with it. I've personally found that if I am relaxed about it and have some humour, other people relax too – but this does depend on the individual.'

HR Accommodations

When someone with profound hearing loss is about to be interviewed or is about to start working at your organisation, it's best to have an open conversation with them. Ask what works for them and how they want the information shared with others in the team. Everyone is unique and will have their own preferences, but Iona suggests that the following are all worthy of consideration:

- Set the context of the conversation before you start. Lip-reading is seventy per cent guesswork, and so understanding the main subject matter is essential.
- Look at the person and talk at your normal pace, as speaking slowly can distort your lip pattern and hinder lip-reading. Try not to cover your mouth with your hand, or rest on your hand and distort your normal expressions.
- If you have a strong regional accent, check for understanding.
- It might be obvious but needs saying: if you're wearing a mask or other mouth covering, please find a way to safely lower it. If not possible, revert to pen and paper or text.
- A speaker with thin lips, a beard or someone who smiles whilst speaking can prove difficult to lip-read.
- Be ready to repeat things that you say and if there is something that your colleague is struggling with, think of another way to say it using different words, as it may be easier to lip-read different words.
- Numbers can be difficult; for example, thirteen and thirty can get mixed up, as well as fifteen and fifty. If unsure, write it down and share it that way.
- At an interview or during a panel discussion, put name cards in front of the speakers. This will reduce the embarrassment of not correctly lip-reading a name.
- If you are presenting a slide deck and have speaker notes, please give a set to your colleague in advance.
- If you are using video conferencing, check for understanding, use the chatbox option to highlight key issues, and enable voice to text where it is of decent quality, or hire an interpreter (either signing or someone who can type speech to text in real time).

- Some colleagues with profound hearing loss may be able to read sign language, but not all are confident. Avoid making assumptions.
- If your colleague is speaking to you and you are struggling to understand them, do not be embarrassed, let them know, and they will try a different way to communicate with you, perhaps using different words or reverting to pen and paper when needed. People who have had hearing loss from an early age have never heard how a word should sound and can only 'hear' the vibrations of their throat inside their heads.
- If your colleague is speaking too loudly, let them know, as they may not be aware. If you are meeting other people, it might be an idea to have a secret prompt you use to help them adjust their speaking level without embarrassment.
- If you are working with a sign language interpreter, look at your colleague and not the interpreter, even though the person themselves will be watching the interpreter. When the interpreter is voicing what the person has signed to them, continue to look at the person rather than the interpreter.
- At larger events and gatherings, the background noise might overwhelm someone who relies on a hearing aid. Find the best place for your colleague and make sure they can sit next to friends or close work colleagues who can support them as needed.
- In an office environment, see if their desk can be backed to a wall, so they can always see someone approaching them, and well away from machines that create noise, such as shredders, photocopiers or drinks machines and kettles. Good lighting will help prevent shadows from falling on the faces of people your colleague is trying to lip-read.
- Some people need the support of an interpreter, captioner or other specialist communication support. They will have had some good and bad experiences. Where possible, allow them to introduce supporters they have successfully worked with before.

- If there is a major organisation announcement (for example, change of personnel, takeover, acquisition, redundancies), please ensure that your colleague gets a private briefing or transcript soon after the meeting, as well as access to appropriate communications support at the meeting.
- When you're doing fun stuff, always think through the ways that you can make your colleague feel included ahead of the event. If it's a quiz, can you have question sheets ready or a slide deck to accompany the quizmaster? If it's a meal out, think about the best place to sit to see most faces and how best to make menu choices in advance, so that any questions can be resolved away from the hubbub of a busy restaurant. If it's an escape room activity or similar, talk to the event hosts well ahead of time, as they may need to get their head office on the case to ensure that everyone is included.
- Help find the best way to handle incoming phone calls. There are textphone systems (aka minicom) and relay services (where an operator transcribes text from the caller in real-time), but all are dependent upon an IT person organising firewalls and, in some cases, providing analogue cabling.
- Ask IT to meet your colleague on day one and help them choose appropriate additional devices or software, as often, the IT team will have blocked employees from adding their own software to a work laptop. Fitting hearing loops in meeting rooms and other key places might well be useful, as well as a portable receiver transmitter system.
- Provide a vibrating pager that activates when the fire alarm is set off and alert the fire marshal.

Further Resources

Useful resources include RNID for general information, support for employers, support for employees, deaf awareness, equipment, support with Access to Work:

https://rnid.org.uk/information-and-support/work/recruiting-people-with-hearing-loss/

Hearing Link for general information and equipment: https://www.hearinglink.org/

Connevans for an excellent range of equipment. Iona says, 'This would be my first port of call to buy any hearing-related equipment (personal or work). Their knowledge and customer service is exceptional, and they are very helpful.'

https://www.connevans.co.uk/catalogue/11/Deaf-Equipment

MyClearText is a company that provides remote captioning on a one-to-one basis for meetings and training. They can also provide onsite captioning. Iona says, 'They have really improved the quality of my working life over the last few years.'

https://mycleartext.com/

28

Heart Block and Pacemakers

Teresa was diagnosed as a child with rheumatic fever and kept under review until she was discharged at sixteen. She was always aware that her heart beat at a slower pace than normal, and she would sometimes feel faint or lose energy, but it wasn't until she was in labour with her second child that she realised just how serious her condition was. Her doctor told her afterwards that her heart had nearly stopped, the diagnosis being 'complete heart block'. Where most people have a resting heartbeat of around sixty to one hundred beats per minute, Teresa's was as low as twenty-five when she was asleep and forty when awake.

Having been diagnosed with heart failure, Teresa was fitted with a pacemaker. As with other surgical operations, she had to rest for several weeks whilst she recuperated, and even when recovery was complete, she had to be careful for a long time about lifting anything heavy, including her rapidly growing baby. Her first pacemaker lasted for seven years and her second for eleven years; they have remarkable batteries. Whilst it shows just like a matchbox under her skin, it is all but invisible when wearing normal office clothing, meaning that sometimes Teresa has to tell people about her pacemaker when she can't do something that would normally be expected of her.

As a wearer of a pacemaker, Teresa can't hold a phone on her left side where the pacemaker is embedded. She has to stand clear of induction hobs and microwaves. She can't look under the bonnet of her car. She has to go around the security monitors at airports (carrying a pacemaker card to help convince security). She can't enter a dry heat sauna, and she has to cover up her scar when sunbathing. She can't have an MRI scan, and general anaesthetic is an issue. At work, she can't enter the IT server room or crawl under her desk to sort out wiring problems. And the good news? Despite the fact that Teresa can't play contact sports, she has run a marathon with her pacemaker!

HR Accommodations

Teresa offers the following advice to organisations trying to be more inclusive:

- When first diagnosed, please provide additional support, possibly in the form of counselling. At an early age, it is all too easy to catastrophise a diagnosis of a failing heart and suddenly become aware of your own mortality.
- Provide lots of opportunities for communication. Keep in touch, talk about the pacemaker and accommodations that will be needed, and ensure that immediate co-workers are aware.
- Don't wrap the person in cotton wool. Provide the support that is wanted or needed, but don't go over the top and make it a big issue.
- Wearing a heart pacemaker is classified as a disability, so don't ignore it just because it is hidden.

Further Resources

https://www.bhf.org.uk/informationsupport/treatments/pacemakers

https://www.pacemakerclub.com/

29

Hodgkin Lymphoma

Wilma was nineteen years old, and she was ill. Alongside a nasty case of what she believed to be flu, she also had crusty mouth sores and a painful neck. The lymph node in her neck grew in size and was to remain enlarged for the next ten years. After the illness, which her GP dismissed as a viral infection, she kept getting fevers, she kept getting tested for glandular fever with negative results, and she kept getting told to rest until she had recovered.

A few years later, Wilma was working, and she would barely get to lunchtime before becoming exhausted and needing to rest or go home. Her employer provided private healthcare and, after a phone call to them, she was referred to an Ear, Nose and Throat (ENT) specialist. After an inconclusive needle biopsy and an ultrasound scan, it was decided that the lymph node in her neck should be removed.

The morning after the operation, when Wilma should have been lying in bed recovering, she woke at 6.30 am and felt ready to go. Her skin had changed from an ashen grey to a pink glow, her mind was alive, and she felt great. The lymph node that had been removed was analysed, and Wilma was shocked to hear that she had been diagnosed with Hodgkin lymphoma: a rare form of cancer that develops in the lymphatic system. She says that she remembers very little of what was said by her consultant after hearing the suffix '-phoma'.

The young team at work were equally shocked. Wilma was only thirty-four, and no one had any experience of this. But they were caring and supportive while Wilma took time off to meet her assigned haematologist and to begin a gruelling series of chemo and radiotherapy that was to last for six months. She received flowers, cards and updates from the team. Conversations at work began to change, and there was an expectation that she would return to work soon after finishing her treatment.

At this point, Wilma was advised that if she did not return to work, her sick pay would be withdrawn. The company income protection scheme was not extended to Wilma, and so she headed back to work. She later learned this was a gap in the absence process. The scheme should have been offered to her and would have enabled her to fully recuperate after her illness and treatment.

Reluctantly, Wilma returned to work part-time, but soon found her line managers had unrealistic expectations about how quickly she would be able to ramp up to full-time hours. She couldn't understand how someone could phase back from maternity leave over twelve weeks, and yet she, a cancer patient, was expected to phase back to full-time hours over four weeks.

Wilma's confidence was low. Her hair was thin and wispy, and she felt like she had been demoted during a restructuring that occurred whilst she was away. A simple request to move her desk was refused, and she found it difficult to be positive. Looking back, she knows that she was having a mental breakdown, something that is common with people who have gone through such a life-changing experience. There was no thought at the time for her mental wellbeing and what support she may have needed to come to terms with the months that had just passed. It didn't help when one of her colleagues confided in her that she had undergone counselling before she could talk to her because she was so scared of getting cancer herself. As Wilma says, you only find out who your real friends are in a crisis.

She also suffered the indignity of being given a poor performance rating by her manager. She had this overturned through a grievance, but she should never have had to go this far and remains concerned that others in a similar situation would not have the mental or physical strength to mount the challenge.

HR Accommodations

Wilma offers the following thoughts to line managers of people undertaking treatment for Hodgkin Lymphoma:

- Throw the sickness absence rule book out of the window.
- Find time to read up about and understand cancer and its treatments at a deeper level.
- Show empathy and compassion, and listen to the person. Find ways for them to keep in touch that work for them whilst undertaking treatment.
- On return to work, agree sensible and appropriate phasing back. Remember that they will probably be exhausted at first.
- Find opportunities for flexible home working.
- Remember that their systems are immunocompromised after treatment. Do not expose them to unnecessary risk (e.g. if flu is making the rounds at work).
- Ensure that the person, and possibly co-workers, have access to counselling support. Helping someone with their mental welfare can be key to their return to full productivity.

Further Resources

https://www.cancerresearchuk.org/about-cancer/hodgkin-lymphoma

https://www.macmillan.org.uk/cancer-information-and-support/lymphoma/hodgkin https://lymphoma-action.org.uk/

See Also
Breast Cancer
Prostate Cancer

30

Highly Sensitive Person (HSP) aka Sensory Processing Sensitivity (SPS)

Research in the 1990s identified that between fifteen and twenty per cent of the population were far more sensitive to physical, emotional and social stimuli than the rest. In Elizabeth's case, this means that she experiences things with far greater magnification than others: one person's sadness can be her deep sorrow, and joy can translate as ecstasy; smells that to most are unpleasant can be overwhelming; scenes of violence or death on a TV programme can have a long-lasting impact. These symptoms should not be confused with introversion or gender: in the academic studies, about thirty per cent of HSPs were extroverts, and the male/female ratio was balanced.

Elizabeth has an overactive mind. She thinks deeply and strategically about many things, often over quite long periods, returning to them with greater understanding. She brings many useful talents to the workplace that others do not possess, including her intuition and empathy for situations and people. She can walk into a room or meet a person and gauge what is going on within a matter of minutes. For her, being an HSP can lead to frustration in both life and work when her opinions are ignored because others have not sensed what is going on, or she sees people making snap decisions based on little evidence or insight. If something bothers her, then she will have difficulty sleeping. Often the only way to resolve it is to switch the laptop back on and write and send the email or answer the query, regardless of the time of night.

Elizabeth was aware from a young age that she was more sensitive than the rest of her family and friends. Some clowns moulded into her cot had to be sawn off to prevent her from being terrified at night and, when staying away with relatives, she would dread things like a trip to the toilet when it was dark. She was often told to 'toughen up' or 'stop taking everything to heart'.

To counter some of these sensitivities, Elizabeth has developed strong spiritual beliefs, which give her a framework for her life decisions. She is driven and feels that she works harder than her colleagues, even if this isn't always appreciated. In her career particularly, she has often felt misunderstood by her managers, who are different to her and do not make any effort to understand her talents.

HR Accommodations

To help accommodate an HSP in the workplace, Elizabeth suggests:

- For someone to tell you that they are highly sensitive is a big step in itself; many prefer not to speak out openly in public. Listen to how it affects them and ask questions to understand how best you can help.
- See the person for who they are, learn their strengths and play to them.
- Allow for flexible working hours. They may need to sleep in the morning after working all night on something that troubled them. When they do work, it is likely to be intense and productive, making any allowances worthwhile.
- When an HSP tells you they have a hunch about something, hear them out. It is probably based on many facts that they have put together and analysed; it is not simply gut instinct.
- If there is to be work carried out in an office environment (e.g. drilling or repainting), you may need to allow the HSP to work at

home. They will find it hard to work with that noise being amplified in their minds. Smells may also prove overpowering. Even someone eating something at their desk can lead to issues.

Further Resources
https://hsperson.com/
https://www.verywellmind.com/highly-sensitive-persons-traits-that-create-more-stress-4126393

See Also
Attention Deficit Hyperactivity Disorder (ADHD)
Rejection Sensitive Dysphoria (RSD)

31

Human Immunodeficiency Virus (HIV)

It started with an upset stomach, sickness, diarrhoea, high fever and chills. This was followed by night sweats that were so severe that the duvet had to be changed. The fever grew, accompanied by a nasty cold and headaches and chills that Artic says felt like someone was blowing freezing cold air through his bones. Think of flu on steroids that lasts for ten days. However, unlike flu, where the symptoms often reduce slowly over many days, Artic explains that his symptoms rapidly disappeared.

This initial period is known as the seroconversion phase. It is the time when the body is fighting against the virus (initially, this is the acute phase) and is only just beginning to create antibodies.

Artic realised that his symptoms occurred about two weeks after he had unprotected sex with someone with unknown HIV status. The human immunodeficiency virus was now systematically destroying his CD4 white blood cells, causing all the above symptoms. To confirm that it was HIV and not another virus, Artic took a blood test at a specialist clinic, where they gave him emotional and psychological support before revealing that he was HIV positive. Further detailed tests followed, alongside daily phone calls to check how he was doing, both physically and mentally.

Having been diagnosed, the first thing that Artic needed was deep emotional support from his friends. Whilst he knew that medicines would be able to reduce the impact of the virus, he also knew that he would now be reliant on drugs for the rest of his life to counter the virus and allow the CD4 cells to get back to normal levels.

Artic was aware of the lack of understanding in the wider community, even the stigma associated with being HIV positive. Many people believe that you have to keep away from someone with HIV, whereas the reality is that the virus only has a short life span outside the body and can't be passed on through saliva, sweat or urine. Its routes of transmission are limited to anal or vaginal sex without a condom, sharing needles and from mother to child during maternity.

Whilst having sex with someone who is suspected of being HIV positive can now be treated with a post-exposure prophylactic drug (PEP), provided that it is within twenty-four hours, this wasn't available to Artic, and so began a series of regular appointments at the clinic. Artic's blood was tested every two weeks to measure the viral load, and on the back of this information, the doctor prescribed a combination of anti-retroviral drugs. The treatment aims to bring the viral load down to an undetectable level so that it ceases to damage the body and the patient can live much more normally, given that it is no longer transmissible at these low levels. Getting to that lower level takes between three and twelve months, and in this way the condition can easily be considered 'hidden'. Artic says a term that is currently being used is U=U (undetectable equals untransmittable).

Untreated HIV infection leads to AIDS (Acquired Immunodeficiency Syndrome), which is when the CD4 cells, also known as T Cells, are killed off to the point where the body can't keep infections at bay. Today the number of people with AIDS is much smaller than when the virus was first identified and treated.

HIV medication can have side effects. A common reaction a week to ten days after treatment begins is a severe rash over the whole body that needs creams, and often steroids, to control. In a small number of people, the medicine binds with the HIV, making larger molecules for the liver to clean out, causing liver problems. Regular blood tests monitor for this, and the usual response by doctors is to change the combination of medicines until they find a set that the patient tolerates.

The NHS notes that over 100,000 people in the UK live with HIV, ninety-seven per cent of whom are on medication to suppress the virus. Perhaps due to the pandemic, 2020 was a record year for both low infections and increased testing.

As Artic says, people who live with HIV don't need to act differently, keep their distance, or take care not to breathe on someone close by (the old myths of catching HIV by sharing a drink, coughing, sneezing, hugging or being infected by insects are all untrue; in so many ways it's *not* like Covid). Instead, the problem for the HIV patient is the stigma: the lack of understanding shown by others, and the fear of rejection, loneliness and isolation from friends, family and loved ones. Throwaway comments, like being 'dirty' or 'riddled', leave big wounds.

HR Accommodations
Artic offers the following advice for the work environment:

- It's not a legal requirement for a colleague to disclose their HIV status, and most people won't for fear of repercussions. However, if a colleague has the courage to tell you they are HIV positive, sit and listen, and show them the empathy and care that they need.
- Talk to them about their medication and ask about likely side effects and things you might need to support them.
- If it feels appropriate, hug them, and tell them that you have their back. Fighting the stigma and providing emotional support is going to be key for their mental health on the road ahead.
- Make flexible provisions so that they can attend clinics and take confidential calls as and when needed, without having to keep supplying potentially embarrassing notes. If necessary, amend any automated absence management system to stop them from being referred regularly for review.

- Your colleague might be more susceptible to common colds and flu. If this is the case, consider allowing them to work from home and reduce the risk of infection whilst their immune system is in recovery.
- Some people experience fatigue and short-term memory loss whilst on the initial medication; allow for this in any performance-related management programmes.

Further Resources
https://www.tht.org.uk/
https://positivelyuk.org/
https://www.nat.org.uk/

32

Hydrocephalus

Twenty-three-year-old Andrea was in the second week of her second job in HR when she developed a headache that got progressively worse. She was prescribed migraine tablets, but the next day she went to A&E because the pain was excruciating. The emergency team were puzzled; she had a neck ache and was heavily affected by the light, both classic migraine side effects. They ran blood tests, undertook a lumbar puncture and diagnosed viral meningitis. A few days later, Andrea was discharged.

After an awful week where her symptoms worsened, she was re-admitted and taken for an MRI scan, which revealed two brain abscesses. She was moved to a specialist neurosurgery unit, where, unfortunately, one of the abscesses burst and led to six weeks in intensive care, a further nine operations on her brain, and another month in hospital whilst her body recovered.

One of the operations introduced a shunt into Andrea's brain: in essence, a tube that took the excess cerebrospinal fluid from her brain to her abdomen. The importance of this she only discovered when it later became blocked, and she simply didn't wake up. When she did, she was back in ICU. Her company had phoned the emergency services when she didn't attend work and wasn't answering her phones. They probably saved her life.

The tenth operation, to replace the blocked shunt, left a scar that she chose to cover with a head scarf. Ironically, the wearing of the scarf led to a complaint that she looked too casual in the workplace!

Andrea's condition is known as hydrocephalus, which is also known as 'water on the brain' and refers to the accumulation of spinal fluid in the brain. With the blockage cleared, and the shunt in place for life, Andrea now lives with her condition, which is a classified disability. She can never have another MRI scan, ride on a roller coaster or go scuba diving, but she can and has had a baby (with lots of extra care, but all went well). She has continued to build a successful career in HR and has an understandable commitment to ensuring all staff are supported through sudden illness and the longer-term impact on them and family members.

As with so many conditions, the range of symptoms that people have to live with is varied. They include intermittent pain (usually in the head and neck), problems walking and with vision, occasional fainting and nausea. In older patients, forgetfulness and impaired bladder control are regularly reported.

HR Accommodations
Andrea's tips for HR teams are:

- If someone tells you that they have had a brain injury or hydrocephalus, take the time to understand what this means for them and make sure that you have their address, phone numbers and emergency contact details kept up to date.
- If they travel for work on their own, check in with them regularly. If one day they are absent and fail to call in sick, or they suddenly seem unwell, treat this as an emergency and call an ambulance.
- Read up and understand the type of operations and treatment they are receiving. Find out about the possible side effects of any medicines.
- Be ready to be flexible with work projects and working hours.
- Ask their permission to tell work colleagues (or agree that they will tell them), so that anything out of the ordinary can be acted upon.

- Make any other accommodations that are needed for the physical environment, like a special chair or sit-stand desk, which can be particularly useful for someone who suffers from neck pains when leaning over a laptop.

Further Resources
https://www.hydroassoc.org/
https://www.ninds.nih.gov/Disorders/Patient-Caregiver-Education/Fact-Sheets/Hydrocephalus-Fact-Sheet
https://www.headway.org.uk/about-brain-injury/individuals/types-of-brain-injury/hydrocephalus/

See Also
Aphasia
Head Injuries

33

Hypermobility Spectrum Disorder (HSD)

At twenty-three months, Gill's daughter was late learning to walk. Gill had often raised concerns about the position of her daughter's feet with the health visitor and her GP, but was always fobbed off and told she was an over-anxious mum, and that all young children's feet are flat. When her daughter was three years old, she ran across the playground, tripped, and knocked her front tooth out. This led to a series of events that resulted in a referral to a podiatrist and a paediatrician, who diagnosed her daughter with Hypermobility Spectrum Disorder (HSD). During the diagnosis process, a series of tests were used, including the Beighton score, which looks at the hypermobility of joints (such as the thumb bending to lie flat against the forearm). A number of the symptoms of HSD would have been referred to as being 'double jointed' in the past. As her daughter went through the tests, Gill realised that she could do the same things and that she was also on the hypermobility spectrum.

Given that HSD is an inheritable genetic condition, this made sense, and it started to explain a number of things that had happened to Gill during her life. Gill remembers that she didn't like PE lessons because much of the movement led to pain in her joints, a common issue for people with HSD. The diagnosis also helped explain other concerns that she had raised with her GP, only to be told that everything was in her head. These included episodes of chronic fatigue, allergies to certain medicines and foods, and the startling fact that deep heat treatment made her feel freezing cold rather than hot.

Prior to the diagnosis, Gill's biggest issue had been her pregnancy, which was far from normal. Her body produced an excess of the pregnancy hormone relaxin, which caused Gill to develop acute SPD (Symphysis Pubis Dysfunction – a pregnancy-related condition). To ease her condition, Gill was prescribed a brace to help her body carry the extra weight of the baby and crutches to aid her mobility. Worse was to come. On the advice of her obstetric consultant, Gill was booked in for a caesarean section as a natural birth could cause her already unstable pelvis to split. However, her midwife simply didn't believe her when she tried to explain the amount of pain she was in and that she thought she had gone into labour in the early hours of the morning. As a result, Gill gave birth naturally, quickly and with no pain relief. It was some considerable time after the delivery when Gill's pain levels had not subsided that the doctors realised that her pelvis had indeed split. Unfortunately, by the time this was diagnosed with an MRI scan, it had fused with a growth of bone density where there should be a gap. This means that she lacks the mobility of others and has to think carefully about routes that might include stairs.

Gill has specially made orthotic insoles for her shoes that compensate for her flat feet and ankle pronation and make it possible to walk, but she is still unstable and frequently trips over and falls. She has ongoing high levels of pain, but these can be intermittent and move around her body, so one day her hip might hurt and the next, her elbow. She's been accused of 'faking it' when she limps on the opposite leg after limping on the other one the day before, but this is all part and parcel of HSD. As I was interviewing Gill, she explained that her right shoulder wasn't properly located in its joint (known as a 'sublux' or partial dislocation).

Pain levels also cause Gill to have what she calls 'brain fog' when she just can't concentrate, think clearly or remember things. Gill has developed a reputation for coming out with amusing 'Gillisms' (words that have got confused between her brain and mouth and sound like nonsense). Fortunately, she is blessed with a great sense of humour and manages to laugh most of these off.

Gill has twenty-five per cent hearing loss in both ears and tinnitus, typical traits of HSD. Symptoms can be intermittent, and many medical professionals still do not fully understand the condition, its variables or how to best support people with it.

Life is made more tolerable by the award of a blue disabled badge. This means that when Gill parks, she can push the car door fully open and swing her legs round to the standing position. This reduces the prospect of her pelvis separating, not something that the majority of us have to think about. But when she stands and walks into the office or shop, she will often get accusatory stares and tuts from people who expect to see a person using a wheelchair to prove they are disabled. Indeed, just getting the badge was a battle: the standard tests are all about the lack of mobility in joints, not hypermobility!

Another saving grace is that the organisation Gill works for has an outstanding ethos about supporting disability to ensure they are fully inclusive. They understand that some disabilities are hidden and find solutions specifically tailored to meet individual needs. Her line manager and the HR team have listened, read up and understood what is happening and go out of their way to make things as easy as possible for Gill. For example, when she is needed in the office, they reserve her a desk in the corner (so background noise is limited, and she can hear better), and they provide her with an additional laptop so that she doesn't have to carry the one she uses for home working.

Gill occasionally needs to get from one building to another for meetings with little turnaround time. At first, this caused Gill significant pain and increased falls, heightening anxiety, often meaning that even if she made it to the next meeting on time, she was exhausted and brain fogged. Her line manager recognised that this didn't need to be the case, and with a little forward planning and flexibility, Gill's situation and ability to work to her potential were easily addressed. Checks were made that parking would be available, and all her meetings were arranged for one day in one place so that she didn't have to keep going back in or move – and risk tripping – between buildings.

HR Accommodations

Gill notes the following things which will make it easier for someone with HSD to feel included at work:

- The most important thing you can do is remember that this syndrome affects everyone in a different way, and can affect one person in a different way on different days/times. Maintain an open dialogue and talk through what is best for the person. Be prepared to listen and review the arrangements.
- Flexible hours and days make it easier to work at times when there is no brain fog.
- Interviews and meetings are best held at ground floor level near the entrance next to the disabled parking.
- Handrails on ramps and stairs should be in place, but in older buildings might need to be modified.
- If the work environment requires shoes to be removed, remember that someone like Gill will have real difficulty moving around.
- HSD pain is hidden. It can be managed with strong medicines, but these can have a dulling effect on the brain and on personality, so make appropriate allowances. Many people with HSD have intolerances to medications and so have to rely on prevention of injury rather than cure.
- Support periods of anxiety and depression that some HSD people get with the appropriate empathy and support mechanisms.
- Engage other work colleagues in an appropriate conversation, helping them understand HSD and that they know how to respond if the person trips and falls or if there is a building evacuation.
- Think about seating plans for larger meetings and conferences, and reserve the best seat for access and mobility.

- If your office practises hot-desking, make an exception. Select an appropriate location and keep it reserved.
- Include hearing loops in meeting rooms where possible.
- Provide the key to the accessible toilet.
- Think about office parties and outside events in advance. Often the hosts will have special arrangements that they can put in place to make it an enjoyable day for everyone, regardless of their condition.

Further Resources
https://www.hypermobility.org/
https://www.ehlers-danlos.com/assessing-joint-hypermobility/

See Also
Ehlers-Danlos Syndromes

34

Hypersexuality

Sakura had her first crush on her form tutor on arrival at secondary school, having raced through puberty at junior school. She recalls having a strong sex drive in her early years, even though she didn't have sex until she was fourteen. Her first experience was 'disappointing'. The boy was two years older than her but was 'clearly inexperienced', and this led Sakura to hunt for someone that could satisfy her needs. Within a year, she had formed fleeting relationships with a series of boys and young men. Parties were her best source, and she learned just how easy it was to seduce men and get them to do her bidding.

Going to university was her ambition, fuelled by the thought that she would be able to meet many more men away from home. At last, she would be able to do what she wanted, when she wanted, rather than skirt around her mother (her father had left many years before). Throughout this period of her life, she had a weekend job at a pharmacy and was able to ensure a steady supply of condoms, the only thing she always insisted on (although she jokes that breath freshener was added after a while!). University lived up to her best hopes, and with time and the assistance of alcohol, she discovered that she was equally comfortable sleeping with men and women.

What relevance does this have to the work environment? Having completed her three years at university, Sakura landed her first role as a trainee at a utility company. She joined eleven other graduates, who were to spend two weeks in a country hotel for their induction and bonding. At the end of the first week, the People Director visited the hotel and asked to see Sakura. He told her that he had received four complaints of sexual harassment made against her. Sakura was shocked. It was a wake-up call now that she had left college and was now a corporate citizen. She wanted to keep her job.

Up until that point, Sakura had merely thought of herself as promiscuous and that 'my body was mine to enjoy'. Her People Director helped her understand how her actions were negatively impacting her colleagues. She says that he was sensitive and supportive, and once she had accepted that she was behaving outside the acceptable norms of the workplace, he said he would arrange for her to receive appropriate therapy.

On Saturday afternoon, she apologised to the whole group and helped them understand that she had meant no harm. The conversation was positive, and the group accepted her sincerity. The complaints were withdrawn. Indeed, by the following Tuesday, the trainees were trying to persuade her to engage more with the group in the way that she had before her warning.

A few weeks after the training programme ended, Sakura met a psychologist that the company recommended and paid for, and was later diagnosed as having an unusually high sex drive, termed hypersexuality (previously known as nymphomania). She rejected hormone therapy, both fearing the side effects and knowing that she would want to start a family at some point in the future, and instead opted for a series of consultations.

Fast forward ten years, and Sakura has recently joined a new virtual utility company in a senior role. She attends a bimonthly meeting with her psychotherapist and regularly chats with other women who share her condition on a Facebook group. She has chosen not to disclose her condition to her new company: she feared that if she raised it during the selection process that she would be discriminated against, and having joined, she has not yet felt comfortable enough to talk to her line manager or the HR team about it.

So far, Sakura has been able to suppress her urges but explains that they are still strong. She explains that the most difficult moments are when she is either in a room alone with someone that she finds attractive or when she is going for drinks with the team after work. To maintain control, she has told her colleagues that she has a low tolerance to alcohol, and now nobody bats an eyelid when she has a mocktail whilst they drink the bar dry.

In thinking about what people can learn from her condition, Sakura says that the approach taken by her first company was exemplary. The fact that she wasn't judged for her behaviour but instead offered appropriate support and help, just when she needed it, gave her the chance to understand herself better and turn her life around. Reflecting back to her first encounter with the People Director, she feels that she might not have fared so well if she was male and hopes that everyone reading this account handles each case in as fair and reasonable a way as possible, regardless of gender.

HR Accommodations

Sakura understands that her condition is largely hidden and not considered to be a disability, but she does suggest that an HR team that becomes aware of someone with this condition does not treat them as a sex pest, but instead as someone who has biological needs that are not as easily satisfied as most members of the team. Being supportive and accepting that the person might need help to find the appropriate balance in the workplace is probably best referred to an occupational health physician or psychologist, who will provide a treatment plan, or help in keeping to it.

Further resources

www.mayoclinic.org/diseases-conditions/compulsive-sexual-behavior/symptoms-causes/syc-20360434

35

Hypothyroidism

Hypothyroidism is the term given to a person whose thyroid gland is not producing enough hormones, which in turn leads to a number of functions in the body slowing down. This can include metabolism and can result in weight gain. Tiredness and depression are symptoms that are regularly reported to doctors where the thyroid function is known to be compromised. It is a lifelong condition and usually gets progressively worse. Currently there is no cure, but symptoms can be compensated for by taking daily thyroxine tablets. Other symptoms can include being sensitive to both low and high temperatures, and regularly suffering from constipation. Many people develop mobility issues due to the weight gain they experience, combined with fatigue.

Jules's Experience

Jules was twenty, a self-styled 'working-class Yorkshire lass' and enjoying life at university. She started to feel unusually tired over several weeks; she put on weight, her face became more puffy than usual, and a grey stripe developed in her hair. Sensibly, she went to her campus GP, who ordered blood tests. The diagnosis was that she had an underactive thyroid and needed to take hormone replacement tablets (levothyroxine) for the rest of her life, there being no other means of treatment currently known to the medical profession. No further investigations, no referral to an endocrinologist, no discussion – just a repeat prescription and away she went.

Jules had always been prone to anxiety and occasionally to periods of depression. When she was younger, she put this down to growing up. She now knows that these are symptoms often linked to hypothyroidism. To help her deal with these episodes, her doctor prescribed a combination of antidepressants to help alleviate her anxiety and improve her sleep, together with a programme of CBT (cognitive behavioural therapy).

Jules gets tired occasionally, especially in the late evening, and confesses to being a bit whingy, but she doesn't suffer as badly as some do from the other common symptoms of sleep loss, fine hair, dry skin, sensitivity to the cold and heat, and muscle aches. She does her best to follow the current advice, which includes keeping hydrated whilst eating as little gluten as possible and ensuring at least a two-hour gap between taking her thyroid medication and consuming caffeine or iron supplements, which can inhibit absorption. She has to choose when to drink alcohol because it gives her terrible hangovers.

Having lived with hypothyroidism as a police officer, a manager at Stonewall, and now as the co-founder of The Inclusion Initiative, Jules is now happily married, pregnant, and, instead of her annual blood tests to ensure the right hormone levels in her blood, she is being tested regularly to ensure that the baby is well looked after.

Jenny's Experience

When it all started, Jenny says that she remembers not feeling great, that she was more fatigued than she should have been. Being young and living a full life she dismissed it at first, but when she started to have exceptionally heavy periods, as well as limp hair and dry skin, she approached her GP, who recognised her symptoms and tested her thyroid function.

Jenny was struggling to get out of bed in the mornings, and even moving from the sofa to the bedroom in the evening 'felt like climbing Everest'. She wasn't feeling her bubbly self nor enjoying life as she should. Tests were run, and she hit a thyroid score that was literally off the chart in the thirties when the 'normal' range is between 0.4 and 4. Her GP actually phoned her at work to give her the results; they were so far off the scale.

The following eighteen months were trial and error: taking the tablets, going for blood tests, altering the tablet strength, more tests until finally getting it right. During the early days, Jenny's periods were heavy and painful, some of her hair started to fall out and her energy levels dropped to an all-time low.

And now for the good news. The tablets are working at the right level and Jenny has her life under control. She has a great sense of humour and has started to make progress in HR after self-funding her own CIPD programme.

HR Accommodations

Jules and Jenny have this advice for HR teams to provide the best environment for someone with hypothyroidism:

- When someone explains that they have been diagnosed with Hypothyroidism, take time to sit and listen to how it is affecting them. It's different for everyone, so find out what is important for them.
- Be ready for a lengthy adjustment as the doctors find the right level of support for the individual. Agree to a flexible work schedule whilst the employee is adjusting to the required levels of thyroxine for their body. This could mean reduced hours until the fatigue is better managed or time to attend regular blood tests for the thyroid reading until the medication is at the required level. It takes six to eight weeks for the medication to take effect, so expect blood tests after each change in medication levels. During the period of adjustment, it might be worthwhile allowing flexi-time so that if fatigue or migraine hits in the morning or the afternoon, an employee is 'free' to adjust their day.

- Discuss with the person whether they would be willing to let close colleagues at work know about their condition, educating them as needed, and helping them understand that there may be issues with the regular need to visit the bathroom or to open/close windows or adjust heaters.
- Providing a quiet room or private space at work, especially one that can be dark in the middle of the day, can be helpful for times when the person needs to recharge their batteries.
- Computer screens can be a problem, especially longer-term: things like a filter can help, as can blue light filters on prescription screen-reading glasses, as well as techniques like dimming or inverting the screen (white text on a black background).
- If your colleague struggles with the workplace temperature, see if there is a better place for them to sit than in the direct path of the heater/aircon unit.
- Ensure that tea and coffee points have gluten-free snacks in the machines and caffeine-free alternatives for hot drinks.
- If your colleague does catch a cold or a virus, remember that it's best they fully recuperate first. If they try to rush back, they may end up being ill and less productive for longer.
- Post pandemic, allowing your colleague to work from home several days a week will pay dividends; they won't have to commute and will be able to do so much more without being unnecessarily tired.

Further Resources

https://www.btf-thyroid.org/
https://www.btf-thyroid.org/hypothyroidism
https://www.british-thyroid-association.org/
https://thyroiduk.org/
https://www.thyroidtrust.org/
https://www.eurothyroid.com/

36

In Vitro Fertilisation (IVF)

Childlessness is different to being childfree, which, like becoming a parent, is a life choice. Infertility issues affect one in five women, significant numbers of males, trans and non-binary people, as well as those close to the individuals affected. Some people with this hidden condition explore the option of In Vitro Fertilisation (IVF), a medical technique in which an egg is fertilised by sperm outside the body, and then returned to the womb to grow and develop.

Anna's Experience

Anna wanted to talk to me about her experience to help others understand this hidden condition. Anna has a superb employer and a loving husband; the perfect combination to support a family. After several fruitless years of trying, she and her husband sought advice, and after much testing and prodding, they were told that they had 'unexplained infertility'. This took some getting used to; others have said that it can be easier to live with and understand if there is a diagnosis, even if there is no cure.

Having learned that both Anna's eggs and her husband's sperm were viable, they decided to try IVF. In vitro fertilisation sounds straightforward until you learn some of the details. You start with blood tests, HIV tests, and other health checks. Next comes a series of hormone injections over several weeks to stimulate egg production. Again this sounds simple, but Anna explains that the hormone injections can prove painful whilst they are experimenting with the correct levels. She asked me to imagine being haunted by the dementors in a Harry Potter book to understand how they affect the brain and body.

Close to the expected time of ovulation, daily scans of the ovaries are taken before an appointment at the clinic. Anna recalls that the egg collection itself is a painful procedure. It has to be done under sedation and takes up the best part of a day. Egg collection isn't always successful, but when it is, there follow several days of waiting to see if the fertilisation with the sperm has been successful. If it is, the prospective mother faces another trip into the clinic for the embryo to be implanted in her womb and to be given another hormone through pessaries. Another two weeks pass, and then, after all this time and money (circa £6,000 per cycle in 2020), the feeling of loss that follows when a period starts is probably impossible for anyone who has not been through this emotional and physical roller coaster to understand. After a good number of attempts, Anna and her husband decided that they needed a break from the endless repeating process of hormones, collection, implantation and then bleeding.

Being childless, but not by choice, is a tough place to be. Social media is filled with baby photos and videos of toddlers getting up to tricks. 'Guess the weight of the baby' sweepstakes are all too common in the workplace, as are discussions during a pandemic about the pressure on parents of home working. Every time someone asks, 'And do you have children?' a deep emotional response is triggered that will never go away.

Throughout her time trying to have a baby, Anna's team at work were supportive. She was given flexible working time to be able to make appointments and emotional support when things were tough. Even so, she says that close colleagues at work and friends at home were embarrassed or afraid to talk about what she was going through, or they would say things like 'Have you tried turmeric', or 'Keep trying, it will come good in the end.' As a consequence of her experiences, she encourages everyone to find time to sit and chat and help people going through this as much as they can.

Anna Butcher wrote an insightful blog about IVF, which she has consented to be reprinted in this book:

Gonal and the eagle

Why is there an eagle involved, and who is Gonal? Gonal-f is the name of the drug I'm going to be injecting. Gonal's purpose is to grow eggs via hormones, which I'll inject daily for about twelve to fourteen days, after which D gets involved and does his business into a pot. The eagle is code for my period. I start treatment on days two to four of my cycle, so I've been waiting for the eagle to land all week. I'm eight days late, which is probably due to food poisoning last month and, for the first time in a good few years, wanting the eagle to arrive rather than dreading it. The eagle landed today, so tomorrow, I'll start a short protocol and will have a baseline scan to see how many follicles I have before Gonal works his magic. I'm excited, scared and hopeful all at once.

The first Gonal jab

It didn't hurt in the slightest and slid into my thigh with ease. Since injecting, I've been experiencing imaginary twinges. I'm convinced they are imaginary as it's far too early for symptoms. I feel like something should be happening now, and I'm wondering how the follicles are getting on in there. They could be doing a happy dance or not really noticing. Saturday (our first progress scan) will reveal all. The aim is to grow a decent amount, the majority of which should contain an egg. In a non-IVF month, one follicle matures and an egg bursts out (I imagine it's like a cannon firing.) I don't know what happens to the other follicles; do they shrivel away or just droop like an unwatered plant until the following month when they spring back up? Not to worry, as the point of IVF is to aspirate the biggest follicles with the hope that an egg is hidden inside each one. IVF catches the eggs before the cannon is fired, so it's a bit like emptying out the cannonballs before the explosives are lit. Most women will produce – can anyone think of a better word that doesn't make us sound like poultry? – a few eggs per IVF cycle, although I know of one who produced only one and had a successful pregnancy and another who ended up with twenty and didn't...

Four eggs and a wombat

The title has given away the number of eggs they retrieved. Given my initial number of sixteen follicles, I was pretty gutted that only a quarter managed to create an egg. We also need to have an additional procedure called ICSI, which stands for Intracytoplasmic Sperm Injection. None the wiser? It means the embryologist injects the sperm directly into the eggs, rather than standard IVF, where the eggs and the tadpoles are left to get on with it themselves in the Petri dish. Needless to say, this was all quite disappointing, and I don't mind admitting to spending most of the day feeling upset. But speaking to the family this evening and receiving various messages during the day helped massively.

So where does the wombat feature? If I were to advise anyone else going through infertility and subsequent treatment, I would tell them to stay away from Google. I happened to not take my own advice today and spent a few minutes googling four eggs and ICSI. Having spoken to my brother-in-law this evening, who advised that you can find any outcome on Google, including someone giving birth to a wombat, I've recognised the error of my ways. It did help me tonight, though, in being able to include the full terminology for ICSI, so I'll let myself off slightly.

Tomorrow we find out how many eggs have fertilised, probably the part I've been most frightened of throughout. I'm hoping they call after nine so I at least get a lie-in after a night dreaming of baby wombats.

Two going in, Beryl (egg transfer day)

On Wednesday, the day after egg collection, I found out that two of our eggs had been fertilised. I spent most of Thursday panicking that I would receive a phone call telling me that the embryos had withered away, which resulted in a couple of answered calls to PPI sales companies and the dreaded 'Have you had an accident...' nuisances. Luckily neither call was from the clinic, so I spent most of the day relaxing.

Back to London today (Friday) for our 11 am appointment and back into the glamorous gown. No sedation for this procedure, as it's painless. (What a shame; I can now see the appeal of narcotics, if I'm honest.) I had to have a full bladder, which is a fine balance to achieve as transfers rarely run to time, being much less critical time-wise compared with egg collection. We were in the same room, and I could hear people being wheeled in and out; one lady got eleven eggs! I will admit I was envious. I think we went in at 11.40 am, so you can imagine the feeling of having held my full bladder since before 11 am...

Into the transfer room, legs in stirrups and a gowned D sitting away from the business end, we were good to go. David, the embryologist (a lovely man), came in to join the others in the room. He explained that the embryos were slightly below average quality and behind in their development, which is measured by the number of cells the embryo has divided into. Ours were at five; they would have liked to see between six and nine for this stage, which is why he recommended having two put back in. We both agreed wholeheartedly and signed yet another form, all of this with my legs in stirrups, so not the most dignified of meetings! The transfer process was completely painless and pretty amazing. We saw the test tube containing our embryos being carried in by David, which was cool. The doctors use a screen to see where to insert, all completed in under twenty minutes. The doctor said the transfer had gone well, and everyone wished us the best. After checking that my going for a wee wouldn't push the embryos out, we went home for the dreaded two-week wait.

The two-week wait

In a normal month of trying to get pregnant, the two-week wait following ovulation occupies your mind immensely. After IVF, multiply this by a million. Every twinge, headache, arm ache, leg ache, backache is analysed. The cruellest thing is that obvious pregnancy symptoms like nausea, headaches and stomach cramps can also be attributed to the pessaries I'm using, which I fondly refer to as 'arse pessaries'. I have no shame anymore and have disclosed most details on here, but sorry if you're eating.

This is definitely the hardest part; ask anyone who's been through it, even those who experienced severe side effects from the injections. I would take another fourteen days of injections, another month of scans up the front bit, another agonising wait for the fertilisation phone call, even another egg collection over this. Slight confession: the anaesthetic part of the egg collection was bloody amazing, so no wonder I would take that again.

When you're in the throes of treatment, you have structure and regular contact with medical professionals who support you at every step. Once you leave after embryo transfer, you're on your own, and all you can do is wait. We did receive a lovely email from our clinic reminding us that they are on hand with any questions or support to be offered, as the two-week wait can be a lonely time. This, albeit a copy-and-paste email, is a lovely touch in my view. Not that there's much I can ask beyond when will I feel symptoms? What if I don't? What are the embryos doing at this precise moment? I'm sure the clinic staff would be helpful, but months spent on forums have already taught me the answer to those questions. It's impossible to interpret anything until the end of the two-week wait.

The return of the eagle (the end of the two-week wait)

Driving home on Tuesday night, I think I knew. I played Gary Barlow's 'Let Me Go' four times whilst tearfully navigating terrible traffic. That sounds sombre, but crying is good for the soul in my eyes (which were a bit puffy by the time I got home). Perhaps I did know; it certainly felt like I was saying goodbye to our two embryos. Before I went to bed on Tuesday, I saw a tiny speck of blood. My heart felt like it would beat so hard I might actually faint, but I managed to sleep.

I had planned to work from home on Wednesday to avoid an all-day meeting at work, afraid I would be unable to contribute or be upset in front of a big group. I started bleeding properly at about 9 am, so I called D, who came straight home. We were due to test on Friday. Having phoned the clinic, we were advised to test on Thursday but decided not to spend Wednesday in limbo and that we would test early. Waiting for the egg timer on the test was torture; we were both shaking like the char-

acters in the *Roobarb and Custard* cartoon. We took the test, which tells you in words how many weeks you are if it's positive, e.g. 'Pregnant one to two weeks'. Our result was not to be. In clear black and white, it read 'Not pregnant'. It was a bit blunt; I felt like saying, 'All right, no need to rub it in'. I think I should invent a test which says 'Not pregnant, sorry lovely person. You're going to be okay, though'. Clearblue: if you ever read this, it's my idea, so don't steal it.

I think we went through the seven stages of grief, all in two days:

I: Shock and denial: We lay in bed, not knowing what to do with ourselves and wondering if this had really just happened. No tears, just a numb feeling of disbelief.

II: Pain and guilt: I felt I had let D down and that my news would make our friends and family sad.

III: Anger: I started hiding newsfeeds of people on Facebook who continually post updates of their children's first achievements, like the first baked bean they've eaten and the first time they've raised their left arm. Disclaimer: I realise this makes me sound bitter, and for that, I'm sorry – but it is hard to see, and emotions are unstable after IVF.

IV: Depression and loneliness: Took place during the course of the remainder of the day. I didn't want to tell anyone, particularly my family, as I couldn't bear to think of them being upset.

V: The upward turn: By the evening and a long phone call to my sister, the guru, I felt better. I don't underestimate how hard it must have been for my brilliant sister (and brother-in-law) to live through this with me, particularly given her own experience. Thanks, Mum and Dad, for making us both and bringing us up to be resilient.

VI: Reconstruction: We talked about trying again but giving ourselves time to heal and enjoy life first. Trying again depends on how realistic our chances are; the clinic will be able to give us lots of information and how we might change our treatment for the future and what our options are. We talked about how lucky we are to have such a great support network and how our lives are pretty good. All the messages I received were so helpful in remembering all that is good in our life. A couple of people wrote, 'There *is nothing I can say to make it better', and 'There are no words to ease the pain', but I tell you what, any words of support really meant the world to us this week. Those exact words made it better.*

VII: Acceptance: I think I got to that stage today. I took the official test this morning; this one just had lines, which is much kinder in my view than the 'state the obvious' version. I went to work and proved to myself that I can still function. I saw friends and had a moan with them about life outside of our IVF. This sounds negative but actually it helped to remind me of life continuing outside of fertility.

I'm not kidding myself that it's now all roses in the garden. I still cried to Gary Barlow again on the way home and got a bit teary during the day. I expect some of the stages above will repeat themselves over the coming months, but tonight I'm okay and so is D. There's a saying in the great film, The Best Exotic Marigold Hotel, *which D says is a rubbish quote, but I like it: 'Everything will be okay in the end. If it's not okay, it's not the end.'*

Zoe's Experience

Zoe had always wanted a family and finally got to the point in her career where the timing made sense. Having had no luck in conceiving over many months, she went to her GP and arranged for a series of tests, which took about four months to arrange and resolve. The results showed that she was unlikely to conceive without intervention, and that IVF would be the best route forward. Zoe didn't want her line manager or team to know, and so took holidays for her appointments. (Never assume someone is going for interviews with a competitor when they take half and full days off in a pattern.)

When she was finally booked for the first cycle of IVF, Zoe also decided to take annual leave. Around this time, her division was restructured, and she was given a new male line manager. Compared to her previous female manager, he was much more open and engaging, and she told him what was happening. He immediately made her feel at ease by telling her that she was a 'silly so-and-so' for not having talked about it before and opening up about the fun and games he was having with his own child. He even read up about IVF and was a source of immense support, suggesting to Zoe that she could just 'go and hide' when her first full IVF cycle failed.

About six months later, Zoe tried again, and this time it was much more difficult. She was impacted by the hormonal treatments that accompanied IVF and went through some hard mood swings, becoming tearful one moment and then angry the next. But the pain and agony were well worth it, because the treatment resulted in twin boys, born by caesarean section, who have made the whole experience worthwhile.

HR Accommodations

Anna, Katharine Rogers (Anna's sister) and Zoe suggest the following ways in which you can make people like them and their partners feel more included at work:

- If your colleague tells you about her plans to undertake IVF, be ready to be flexible with work schedules. There will follow a series of clinics, treatments, and then at least a day off both when the eggs are harvested and when they are implanted. Some clinics will occur on a daily basis, as they measure the propensity to ovulate through regular blood tests and follicle tracking, and they will dictate the times that the person is needed to attend.
- Don't be surprised if the usual standards of work slip slightly. The emotional demands of IVF take their toll, and the drugs affect short-term memory. Understand some hormonal changes will likely take place, and be ready to take the person to one side for a quiet chat rather than brandish the disciplinary code if emotions get out of hand.
- Plan with your colleague who will be told and when. Although it is always disappointing when IVF fails, your colleague will need to weigh up the pros and cons of the team knowing or being ignorant, and at which stages. Sometimes being aware can resolve

issues of not understanding why the person is taking off so much time for the clinics.

- Be prepared for failure; it is a common endpoint. Accept that a period or miscarriage can start at any time of the day or night, and that will be a difficult time. Let them take the lead; in other words, be there for them, but don't push the pace of what they want to talk about. Don't push with questions like 'Will you try again?' and be sensitive about the flaunting of other people's babies and children.
- Consider helping with counselling if none is provided (IVF with the NHS does not currently include counselling support).
- Help set up networks for both working parents and aspiring parents.
- Ensure that your maternity policies include IVF treatment and time-off needs.
- Run a seminar for your MHFAs about IVF and its impact.

Further Resources

https://fertilitynetworkuk.org/
https://fertilitynetworkuk.org/life-without-children/
https://fertilityfoundation.org/
https://www.carefertility.com/
http://janijellybean.blogspot.com/2013/03/for-all-women-who-are-not-mothers-on.html
https://lesleypyne.co.uk/helpful-websites/

37

Lipoedema

In the cruel world of the school playground, Nicola was teased about her 'thunder thighs'. And ever since people have given her advice such as 'eat less and exercise more', but it isn't that easy. If only it was...

It all started at puberty when her hormone levels were changing fast. A trigger inside her switched, and deposits of fat built up in her thighs and upper arms, leading to a damaged lymphatic system. She tried her best to live with it, controlling her diet and exercising (karate, kickboxing and running), but the fat kept on building, so she went to her university doctor to get help. Nothing. She simply said she needed to eat less and exercise more.

Skip forward to maternity, and Nicola finally met a doctor who was concerned about her rapid weight gain, which now included her calves. He referred her to a specialist lymphoedema nurse, and finally, lipoedema was diagnosed.

Lipoedema is an adipose tissue disorder, meaning that Nicola's lymphatic system is not working correctly, and adipose tissue (better known as fat) is being deposited in her legs and arms. This causes not only weight gain but also pain throughout her whole body, as anywhere the fat is deposited can cause painful inflammation. Lipoedema can be considered a 'hidden' condition because to the casual observer, suffers may just appear to be overweight and it may be incorrectly assumed that an unhealthy lifestyle is to blame. Nicola has learned that she cannot eat certain foods, like pasta, without an adverse reaction. Often these foods are the very ones that nutrition websites promote, so she has to work to her own diet.

Lipoedema is categorised by specialists in four stages. In Stage 1, there is an increase in fatty tissue, but the skin is still smooth. Stage 2 sees the fat tissue start to be unevenly distributed, with wrinkles or indentations appearing on the skin surface. Stage 3 includes large additional areas when fat extends beyond the normal body shape and becomes less easy to hide with clothing. Stage 4 is where there is excessive fat build up over large areas, and the person struggles to stand or walk and often has to use mobility devices. It is hereditary, and many people have it without realising. Furthermore, many GPs do not yet recognise it, as it is not something they are trained in.

Whilst there is no medicine that can counteract lipoedema, there are some treatments that can help. These include wearing compression socks or tights, undertaking regular exercise that promotes lymphatic flow, eating specific diets such as the paleo diet, liposuction (under consultant guidance, this can help with being able to walk in later stages), and drinking more water than usual to keep flushing the system.

Counselling is often provided for this condition, especially because it affects lifestyle and cannot be resolved by diet or exercise. The mental toll can be vast as you need to overcome stigma and bias as well as the physical impact of the condition on the body. Cortisol has a huge impact on the inflammation in lipoedema, so stress can cause a flare in the condition.

Some people with lipoedema are also affected by fibromyalgia or can share similar symptoms and so can be prone to fatigue and brain fog.

HR Accommodations
Nicola makes the following suggestions for the workplace:

• Once someone has told you that they have lipoedema, ask them how it affects them and how best you can help.

- Be ready to be flexible in your office hours and allow home working, especially during flare-ups, which remain unpredictable.
- Consider providing a reserved parking space near their place of work, even if they do not have a blue badge yet.
- Ask the facilities team to provide a sit-stand desk if possible and both a foot stool and a foot-bike under their table, so they can pedal whilst working and keep the blood and lymph flowing.
- Review whether extra ramps or lifts will be needed to move to key parts of buildings, and ensure there is an evacuation plan in place where needed.
- Provide specialist chairs to support the body and back.
- Offer the key to the disabled toilet and review placement of desk or workstation to allow ease of access. When drinking more water and wearing compression socks, extra visits and extra time is needed, and it can be embarrassing in a general toilet with queues building up.
- If the NHS is not providing counselling support, ensure they have access to your EAP system.
- When in pain, your colleague may be less able to concentrate on work. Make appropriate allowances.
- Review any meeting or occasion where standing for long periods is expected. This just won't be possible.
- Remember that the Access to Work programme through the government can support workplaces with assessments and funding to support colleagues.

Further Resources
https://www.talklipoedema.org
https://www.lipoedema.co.uk/
https://www.nhs.uk/conditions/lipoedema/

38

Long Covid

We are still learning just what long Covid entails, but if you review the list of symptoms that are being recorded by outpatient clinics and the emerging long Covid rehabilitation centres, it's clear that we will have to take it seriously as a new illness to record on our HR systems, and we will need to think about how to help and support those that are returning to the workforce or supporting a loved one at home with the condition.

Long Covid is not related to the severity with which the initial illness impacts the body. Many cases are being reported amongst people who only had mild Covid symptoms when they first had to isolate (commonly bad headaches, loss of taste and smell, and a persistent dry cough).

Long Covid symptoms include fatigue (extreme tiredness), continuing shortness of breath when moving, intermittent chest pain or tightness, 'brain fog', rashes that flare up from nowhere, irregular and difficult sleep, dizziness, joint pain and tinnitus. Any one of these symptoms can lead to someone needing to take time off work, request reduced working patterns or ask for a change in their duties.

Joanna has been qualified to drive HGV vehicles for over ten years. Up until May 2020, she was regularly transporting parcels between ports and depots for a major international shipping company. She worked all through the initial lockdown as a key worker, and that is when she probably contracted the virus. At first, she thought she had hay fever, something that she gets every year when the trees start to flower, but her symptoms included a migraine that wouldn't shift with normal medicines and she was sweating when she slept. She volunteered for one of the early tests that were being made available and got the news that she was positive, and so she signed off sick.

Two weeks later, Joanna was back on the road but remembers starting to feel drowsy at the wheel, just an hour into a long run from Harwich to Manchester. She pulled over at the next rest station and took her caffeine supplements, and managed to get to her destination an hour behind schedule, taking it very carefully. She delivered her load, parked the cab at the compound and registered as sick and unable to make the next trip.

Joanna then spent the next few weeks on the phone talking to various GPs at her community surgery, trying to convince them she wasn't well. She needed their agreement that she could get signed off and receive sick pay from her employer, who was suggesting that she should either send in a doctor's certificate, get back to work or take unpaid absence. She hit lucky on the third call. She spoke to a doctor in training who had a friend that was suffering from long Covid.

Joanna explains that just making the calls and attending the test centre was exhausting. She was struggling to find the energy just to cook for herself, and even that had lost all its pleasure given that her sense of taste was messed up. Many foods smelt of nothing, whilst a few smelt as if they had gone off, even though she knew they were fresh.

Following a physical examination in the surgery (after testing negative for Covid), Joanna was prescribed a mix of antibiotics and migraine-relief pills. She was also referred to a physiotherapist to start working on regaining her stamina, with special breathing exercises to help her rebuild her lung capacity.

Joanna was signed off initially for six weeks, although it was twenty-two weeks before she could return to work. She had to pay for her own physio after the GP sessions ended and is currently using a cycling machine at home to work on her fitness. Her GP suggested reduced hours on her return to work, something that is very difficult as a driver. Her employer has found an alternative for now, and she is driving local vans rather than long-haul lorries, but at some point, she will need the extra money and hours from the longer journeys, just to get back on top of her mortgage payments. She explained that her local trips make her day quite long. She has to keep taking breaks to recover, and so a normal eight-hour shift takes her eleven or twelve hours to complete.

Joanna sums things up by telling me she is thankful that she survived Covid, given that her uncle and aunt both died from it, but feels like she is now only seventy per cent of the person that she used to be. She is worried that she can't do her full job and uncertain about the future. Will she make a full recovery, or will she be like this for the rest of her life? The uncertainty is the hardest thing to live with, and it leaves her feeling down a lot of the time. She is about to ask her GP whether she can receive some counselling support (her company doesn't have anything at the moment).

HR Accommodations

Accommodations are difficult to judge with long Covid simply because it is being reported in so many different formats. Common suggestions emerging from the press and social media coverage include:

- Many long Covid patients are reporting fatigue. Working from home and flexible working patterns will be important to help bring the person back to work.
- Brain fog for many patients suggests that conversations will need to be backed up with emails to ensure that the person fully understands the measures that you are taking.
- Occupational Health practitioners will be keeping close to developments; ensure they are linked in.
- Treat a diagnosis of long Covid by a doctor as a serious condition that needs support. For many, it is as difficult as chronic fatigue or CFS/ME to handle, and it is likely to be classified as a disability.

Further Resources

https://www.thebraincharity.org.uk/how-we-can-help/practical-help/information-advice/a-z-of-conditions/43-l/1078-long-covid

https://meassociation.org.uk/2020/10/me-association-statement-on-the-nice-clinical-guideline-for-me-cfs-and-the-nice-guideline-for-post-long-covid-19/

https://meassociation.org.uk/2021/05/editorial-working-within-limits-long-covid-me-cfs/

See Also

CFS/ME

39

Lupus aka Systemic Lupus Erythematosus (SLE)

In a healthy body, the immune system seeks out bacteria and viruses and destroys them. An autoimmune disease, such as Systemic Lupus Erythmatosus (SLE), causes problems because the immune system turns on its own organs, mistakenly thinking that they are invading the body. In the case of SLE, the joints, lungs, heart, kidneys and brain can be attacked, with some signs also showing on the skin. This is different to discoid lupus, which attacks the skin, and can lead to chronic scaly skin rashes that may look like extreme patches of eczema covering the face, ears, scalp and other parts of the body.

Symptoms include joint and muscle pain, extreme tiredness, skin rashes, headaches, mouth sores, high temperature, hair loss and sensitivity to light. SLE is not contagious and has no cure, but it can be controlled with medication. It can be considered a hidden condition because the appearance of the sufferer can often be outwardly healthy. However, tell-tale external signs of the onset of SLE include a red skin rash, which can occur anywhere on the body, but typically appears over the bridge of the nose and eyes, and looks like a mask in the shape of a butterfly.

The origins of lupus are still not understood, but it appears to be triggered by traumatic events, which can include puberty (especially prevalent in women, but also some men), a major viral infection, too long spent in direct sunlight, the act of childbirth or the onset of menopause. There is still no single blood test that can help identify lupus, and so mild conditions go undiagnosed for many people. Diagnosis occurs through a series of questions that go back over medical and family history, but primarily is based on the combination of symptoms as they present themselves.

Sherry's Experience

In Sherry's case, none of the early signs were easy to identify with one disease or condition. She was in her early twenties and preparing for a major launch at work. She had a feeling of heaviness in her chest and was fatigued. She describes the sensation as feeling like she had an elephant stepping on her chest whilst she was trying to breathe. The doctor referred her for an X-ray of her chest, but nothing showed up, not even asthma, and all the blood tests that were taken at that time proved negative, so she pushed on with work.

Sherry took to sleeping in a sitting position to reduce the pain and struggled at work with limited sleep. After a while, she started to feel feverish with flu-like symptoms, her temperature shot up to over forty degrees and her oxygen saturation levels dropped. She was admitted to the hospital. As they tried to make her lie down for examination, she was screaming in pain, and on this occasion, the X-ray showed a shadow around both her lungs and her heart. When the doctor listened with a stethoscope, he could hear what is termed a pericardial rub: a specific sound caused by rubbing of the pericardium (the protective layer around the heart) against the outer layer of the heart.

The following morning ultrasound scanning showed that the pericardium was inflamed and filled with fluid. An ECG and Cardiac MRI, along with numerous blood tests, were ordered as the junior doctor had a suspicion that it was a natural response to an attack by Sherry's own antibodies. At that time, in late 1999, the Alliance for Lupus Research were pushing for disease recognition. It may well be that Sherry owes her life to their extensive research and marketing campaigns and her doctor's recent training.

Formally diagnosed with SLE, Sherry was horrified when she was told that her life expectancy was age thirty to thirty-five and that she could never have children because the foetus would be attacked by her own immune system. She was also told that chemotherapy would be needed to suppress her own immune system. She was twenty-three years old, about to move home for a new job and was determined that she was going to get the better of this disease and not add to the statistics.

Sherry was referred to a consultant rheumatologist, who prescribed a high dosage of steroids to reduce the inflammation, followed by a series of immunosuppressants, non-steroidal anti-inflammatory drugs (NSAIDs) and anti-malarial medications to try to reduce the impact of SLE. She started to get severe joint pain in her hands, hips and knees and was unable to get out of bed for days at a time. She was so fatigued that even sleep didn't help but, after a while, the cocktail of medicines kicked in. Sherry started her job and was upfront with her new boss. She had to be, just in case she was to go into cardiac arrest or need time off for medical appointments or if the fatigue and flare-ups slowed her down too much.

It is not all doom and gloom, however. Fast forward twenty years to today, and Sherry has a stable medicine regime, is a successful HR Consultant working in London, is mother to a young child and she is supporting others with lupus through various forums. She has participated in numerous medical trials and is currently on a cocktail of five drugs. She still gets the occasional flare-up, for example, where her hands swell and typing becomes impossible. Joint pain follows, but she says that she is thankful that it is manageable. Sherry also occasionally suffers the odd flare of pericarditis, and this is managed with steroids and lots of rest. Anecdotally, she has worked out that the triggers for a flare-up include too much sugar, alcohol, not enough sleep and stress. She therefore eats lots of fruit and vegetables, drinks far more water than most and avoids cake for breakfast.

Emma's Experience

When the Olympics were at their peak in London 2012, Emma was working twelve-hour shifts as a police officer. She kept getting pains in her arms and falling asleep during the short rest breaks in the mobile canteens that were provided for all those staffing the event. She didn't think anything of it and soldiered on. The following year, with work patterns normalised again, the pains were still there, and she was beginning to feel the effect of the cold and wind on the beat. The pain became so bad that she couldn't lift her arms to take off her T-shirt, and she also had some swelling in her ankles.

In May 2013 Emma's GP ordered blood tests, and when they showed low protein levels, she asked her to eat lots of eggs and retest in a month. Emma gained even more weight, especially in her legs, developed a rash on her chest, and her swollen ankles became even worse. She returned to the GP and this time her urine was tested. This revealed her kidneys weren't functioning correctly, so she was referred to a renal consultant, who diagnosed lupus and ordered a kidney biopsy to confirm.

The biopsy required a couple of days in hospital. By then, Emma had gained about two and a half stone in weight, her blood pressure was low, and she was near collapse when she finally saw the consultant. She was kept in hospital and given steroids, autoimmune tablets, warfarin (to reduce clotting) and a diuretic to reduce water retention. She needed two months of rest at home to recover, her hair was falling out and she was euphoric on the cocktail of drugs. Her brain fog meant that she couldn't even watch TV and, there being no cure, she feared death itself. She was in quite a state when visited by someone from work as part of a home visit, but at least it proved to them that she was genuinely ill.

After several months she returned to a desk job after agreement with the Met Police Occupational Health team, working condensed hours and no nights. She started working in training and slowly regained her health by taking medication, exercising, resting and eating sensibly along the way.

Things were going well, and her medication was reduced, and so Emma applied to be a line manager. For this role she was transferred to a new operational team, but sadly they were unaware of her reasonable adjustments when the transfer was proposed, and it was decided she would have to have a desk-based role instead, even though Emma was keen to work on the streets once again. Emma took this role and tried to remain positive and get some experience as a line manager, but then it was decided her unit was to be moved to Sidcup, a whole one-and-a-half-hour commute from where she lived. Clearly, they had not thought this through, and she was left with no option but to resign. She set up as a freelance trainer in mental health, something at which she now excels (and, ironically, delivers training to police officers around this topic).

Emma is currently in remission. She exercises, watches her diet and takes medicines based on regular testing and blood pressure readings to keep it under control. She has had counselling to ensure that anxiety and stress are kept under control, and she has had to shield herself through the pandemic, being vulnerable to infections. Her current medicines include an anti-malarial, which keeps lupus at bay, Ramipril to keep her blood pressure down due to scarred kidney tissues, and she has regular eye tests to ensure all is well.

Aigle's Experience

Aigle was studying for her degree at Leeds university when she started to feel unwell. She was overly tired and had pains in her joints. She had just returned from a trip to the Ivory Coast, and the doctor checked for various diseases, prescribed some inflammation tablets, and so she thought nothing more of it. When she graduated, she fell ill again and, this time, underwent a further batch of tests, which did finally diagnose lupus. Her doctor prescribed chloroquine, a medicine initially developed for the treatment of malaria but later found to be effective with some lupus patients.

There is no cure for lupus, but various medicines prescribed to Aigle over the years have helped relieve some of the symptoms. These include

Ibuprofen to reduce inflammation and strong painkillers like Co-Co-damol to reduce joint pain. Antimalarials mentioned above have been supplemented by steroids, which have had the disadvantage of rapid weight gain. And at the end of 2020, GSK was granted a licence for the use of Benlysta (belimumab) for the treatment of kidneys inflamed by lupus, giving hope to many hundreds of patients across the world.

Aigle has a monthly outpatient clinic with a rheumatologist and occasionally suffers a flare-up. When her lungs are affected, she has to spend some time in hospital before stabilising or when her kidneys need time to clear. She explains that she never knows when or where in her body a flare-up will occur, but it can happen when she is feeling down. She therefore works hard to keep fit and stays as positive as she can.

Aigle understands that her condition can be confusing to her co-workers, who see someone who looks healthy on the outside taking days off. Helping them understand the nature of the condition is a full-time job in itself. One of her biggest issues is facing a long working day after having a night where she has had little sleep because of the pain in her body. On those occasions, she needs to call in and either delay the start of the day or switch days. The pandemic means that she has been asked to shield by the NHS, bringing a new set of issues to the workplace.

HR Accommodations
Sherry, Aigle and Emma make the following suggestions:

- SLE affects everyone in a different way. If an employee tells you they have been diagnosed, start by talking to them and learning about how it affects them and what help or adjustments they may need. Remember that things will change over time as they get used to living with it, and their bodies acclimatise to the medicines being prescribed.
- Remember that once someone with lupus has told you they have the condition, they are protected by employment disability legislation. Reasonable accommodations need to be provided to make

it as easy as possible for them to contribute fully to the organisation.

- Revise sickness absence policies and automated referrals to occupational health for someone with lupus; there is no point in regularly putting them on review because they have had to take a series of days off work. This is a condition that has no cure and no let-up.

- Flare-ups can happen at any time. Allow a mix of flexible working, homeworking and/or sick leave to resolve times when either your colleague can't work or has limited ability to work.

- Ask IT to provide specialist software for dictation to email and Word etc, so that a colleague who wants to work when their hands are swollen can still do so. A larger mouse, ergonomic keyboard and gel wrist support can also help; such accommodations are well established for people with RSI, and a good IT department should be able to respond with a series of options.

- Conduct a Display Screen Equipment (DSE) risk assessment, as well as determining the best positioning of office equipment and furniture to reduce strain on the joints.

- Arrange key meetings for late morning or afternoons. Sometimes your colleague will need to come in late if they wake up with stiff joints and need to undertake stretching exercises first. Keep hours at proper limits and don't expect the person to work into the evening. Training sessions or team meetings over sandwiches at lunchtimes are not sensible; rest is needed to avoid relapse.

- Allow for regular, proper breaks for the person to exercise. Sitting still in one position is not good for the joints. Sit-stand desks can help greatly. Allow the person to get up and have a longer walk at lunchtime.

- Avoid asking the person to work outside for lengthy periods of time where they have to ensure that they are well protected with sunscreen (even in climates like the UK). Equally, working under fluorescent lights for long periods can be problematic.

- Most colleagues with SLE will be defined as clinically extremely vulnerable if they are taking steroids, immunosuppressants and have major organ involvement, and so will shield during pandemics or the flu season, and are often registered as disabled. When illness is doing the rounds at work, suggest the person works from home where possible. People with lupus generally catch a full-scale debilitating virus, whilst others shake it off with a cough or a sneeze.
- If your colleague becomes pregnant, understand that they will attend many more antenatal clinics than normal, as the care team will want to ensure everything goes well. In Sherry's case, she says that her body was at its best during maternity but wasn't so great afterwards when the hormonal impact reduced, and she needed a lot of time to fully recover.

Further Resources

With the right support in place, employees should be able to successfully manage their disease with minimal issues or disruption to their job or workplace. For more information on how you can support your employee who has SLE, click through to:

https://www.lupusuk.org.uk/wp-content/uploads/2015/10/When-An-Employee-Has-Lupus-V2.0.pdf

https://www.lupusuk.org.uk/

https://www.versusarthritis.org/about-arthritis/conditions/lupus-sle/

https://kaleidoscopefightinglupus.org/100-years-lupus/

40

Maternal Deprivation and Childhood Abuse

In the 1950s, John Bowlby developed the early work of Sigmund Freud, studying the effect on a young child of being deprived of their mother, or a mother substitute, following World War II. More recently, this has led to a body of knowledge on Attachment Theory. In essence, it is noted that young children struggle to accept societal norms and therefore rebel or live life outside the normal boundaries if they do not have a constant caring mother in their early years. This can be exacerbated by frequent moves between orphanages, foster or care homes, or the opposite – by staying for a long period with a mother who neglects the child and deprives them of love and affection (often as a consequence of drug misuse or alcohol addiction).

I had the privilege of a frank, open and honest conversation with Jedda, whose father was abusive and whose mother was an alcoholic and had little time for her children. Jedda lived in an area where spells in prison were an occupational hazard, and everyone looked after themselves. Jedda explained that even though she ran away from home and had self-harmed, she still wanted to have time with her mother, always hoping that she would be able to receive the love that she craved.

Although she is not diagnosed with ADHD or autism, Jedda is sure that this runs in her family and that it was probably heightened by the circumstances in which she was brought up, always having to adapt at short notice to changing circumstances, from being abused to being neglected, to a poor early education as a consequence. She believes that the trauma as a child led to her own brain being rewired, something she has discussed at length with her counsellor. Other traits include difficulty with looking at someone she is speaking to, being OCD about cleaning, being deeply affected by media and social media (e.g. getting obsessed with cot death after Anne Diamond talked about her experiences) and possessing a photographic memory.

This toxic mix has given her a clear goal in her adult life: to create opportunities for her children to be well educated, to go to university and live a fulfilling life. And the lovely upside is that she has achieved just this.

Two of Jedda's traits are that she speaks her mind and she cannot tolerate injustice. She tells things how they are, however uncomfortable that makes people feel. In the work environment, this has proven tricky to say the least (she referenced three occasions that she had raised issues with line managers that needed to be resolved, several of which were related to unsafe practices affecting people in care). She cannot stand by and allow managers to dismiss her concerns without proper investigation, and this has led to conflict.

Jedda says that employers want a fully functioning and compliant employee and that they therefore struggle to cope with her occasional inability to focus on a single issue (the ADHD kicking in), or desire for fairness and equity (based on her upbringing). One of her mentors tried to help her by suggesting that she needed to 'play the game', but she knows that is not possible. And when I tried to see the world from her perspective, it made complete sense: if that was me and I had personally suffered so many injustices, I could not then stand by and allow the same horrors to play out for the next generation, especially if my boss was saying that there was no profit to be made from getting involved or investigating. As Jedda says, trauma as a child often leads to empathy as an adult.

Jedda has found some coping mechanisms as follows:

- When she needs to block out thoughts and concentrate, she will put on her headphones and listen to music.
- She has tried CBT (cognitive behavioural therapy) and found some success.
- Jedda plays Scrabble in her head (think of *The Queen's Gambit* and chess).
- She has a mantra that she recalls before talking to senior managers or in interviews: clear my mind, slow down, speak slowly, keep on task.
- Five close personal friends whom she can turn to whenever needed.
- A counsellor who has provided her with free sessions.
- Studying at college and university to make up for her lost education (she now has a degree).

Not only did I feel humbled by talking to Jedda, but I also came to realise what a great asset she would be to any organisation. She has the ability and intellect to be able to achieve the highest office; she has critical and analytical brainpower; she has empathy and understanding; she is driven and highly motivated, and yet she doesn't fit the comfy norm that so many employers are desperate to find purely because she challenges the status quo and says what she thinks.

HR Accommodations

As a consequence of her experiences, Jedda implores all HR people to take whistleblowing seriously, even when the employee fails to give it that title and simply wants to 'raise a concern'. It takes a lot of courage for someone to report an issue, and it is highly likely that there will be something amiss that needs to be properly investigated. If not, then if the current practice is perceived by at least one person as being unfair, incorrect or dangerous, it probably needs to be changed or recommunicated.

In interview panels, we often talk about 'the right chemistry' when making a selection decision. Conformity with established norms leads eventually to mediocrity. We all need to find, nurture and accommodate our own Jedda.

Further Resources
https://www.victimsupport.org.uk/

41

Ménière's disease (Vertigo and Tinnitus)

Wendy was in her late twenties when she experienced her first episode. Getting up from bed, she headed for the bathroom, but as she did so, her head started spinning and she could hardly stand up. She hadn't been out drinking the night before, she wasn't taking drugs, and the sensation was way more pronounced than the experience many people get when they stand up too quickly and feel short-term dizziness.

Ironically, Wendy was due to attend a training course to become an MHFA that day, so she bumped down the stairs on her bottom and phoned her father for help. She knew she had to get to the course and not let her company down. She'd been brought up only to visit the doctor if you were near death, so as she slowly regained her balance, her dad drove her to and from the course.

When it happened again whilst she was on holiday, Wendy took it seriously and went to see her GP on her return home. She was referred to an ENT (ear, nose and throat) clinic and diagnosed with intermittent low-frequency hearing loss. Only later did she learn that she had Ménière's disease: a condition of the inner ear that causes sudden attacks of vertigo (the feeling of dizziness) and tinnitus (a ringing in the ears), as well as a feeling of pressure building up around the ear. It is most often experienced in one ear, but can be both. The cause of Ménière's disease is not known, but may result from a viral infection, a blockage in the ear or an issue with the immune system turning on itself.

Wendy describes what happens when an episode starts. At first, she hears a high-pitched squealing noise, a bit like the sound that victims of bomb blasts or very loud noises describe. The disorientation comes as the 'noise' moves from ear to ear, as if fading the speakers in a car from back to front or side to side. Wendy says that her eyes flicker and she can become quite distraught, but to others in a room, it is an invisible condition that they rarely notice.

Once diagnosed, Wendy began to control the condition with some lifestyle changes such as practising yoga, a low sodium diet, ensuring good sleeping conditions, taking antihistamines (helps with vertigo) and prochlorperazine (reduces nausea).

In the workplace and in her social life, Wendy's issues with her hearing mean that she often struggles to understand what is being said, especially in a restaurant or busy meeting room, and she can't always differentiate who is talking on a teleconference or multiple-person Zoom call. The tinnitus, in particular, can lead to anxiety because she has no control over when it will cut in and scupper something that she is doing. At its worst, it stops her from driving to meetings or going shopping.

As with many invisible conditions, people with Meniere's disease require strong communication between all parties and a willingness to make accommodations alongside appropriate treatment. The condition will have no effect on someone's ability to grow and develop in their career.

HR Accommodations
Accommodations and support that Wendy has appreciated include:

- Line manager: an open and honest relationship has really helped, which has led to understanding and appropriate support in many different circumstances.
- Team calls: her team have all agreed to call in separately during conferences, rather than sharing a microphone, which means that Wendy can always see who is speaking.

- Occasional working from home means that she can more easily manage her circumstances and reduce her anxiety about having to travel.
- The diagnosis is notifiable to the DVLA. However, they appreciate that people need to be able to drive to work, and monitor the situation rather than enforce unnecessary bans.
- CBT: cognitive behavioural therapy was a great help to Wendy, reducing her stress and helping her rationalise her desire to catastrophise her condition after it was diagnosed.
- Flexible working: Wendy has the ability to call in a bad start to the day and make up the hours later that day or on another day. Such flexibility is key to keeping her productive and motivated.
- When in the workplace, Wendy ensures that close colleagues are aware and know what to do if she suffers from an episode: guide her slowly to a safe space, provide water and call her partner or parents.

Further Resources
https://www.menieres.org.uk/

42

Menopause

Menopause is the term used to describe the point in life when a woman's natural ability to conceive a child diminishes and then ceases. Her monthly cycle of periods also comes to an end. It is considered a hidden condition because many women prefer not to speak about it, often due to embarrassment and the assumption that they will be perceived differently by their colleagues. Menopause typically takes place over many months or years, and yet it can be triggered quite suddenly, for example, after chemotherapy or other trauma, including childbirth. For many women, it is accompanied by a range of side effects including irregular periods, heavy periods and spotting; memory and concentration loss; hot flushes and night sweats; headaches or migraines; anxiety, depression and mood swings; a loss of sex drive and more.

Although most women experience menopause in their fifties, some see the change starting before they are forty-five years old. Often referred to as 'early menopause', women are advised to discuss this with their GP because other factors may be in play. It is believed that there is a greater likelihood of women with early menopause also being more susceptible to osteoarthritis and heart conditions. In certain circumstances, a doctor will suggest further tests or a referral to a specialist and/or prescribe hormone replacements or other treatments.

Just a quick look at the symptoms listed above should make it immediately apparent that menopause can have implications in the workplace and that accommodations will need to be made.

Frankie's Experience

I talked to Frankie about her experiences with early menopause (onset age thirty-three) and the arthritis in her feet that accompanied it. She explained that she knew that something wasn't right when, whilst visiting her parents in Spain, she was given a diagnosis by a doctor that her own GP rejected on her return. It took nearly five years to be formally diagnosed, and during that time she experienced many problems.

At work, she was being asked to spend many hours continuously on the sales floor. She explained that she had pain in her feet, but this wasn't taken seriously by her supervisor, and she eventually had to take out a grievance – this created friction with her store manager and continuing difficulties. Without a diagnosis, it was hard to get the support she needed.

Frankie next experienced hot flushes, which she described as an inferno, alongside bouts of feeling very cold and an intermittent brain fog. During one foggy moment, she asked a member of her team to do something that was potentially unsafe, and then later, when her brain cleared, she asked them what on earth they were doing!

As her accompanying arthritis flared up, she increasingly needed to walk with crutches or a stick and to take more breaks to recover from the pain. Frankie's flare-ups and the other symptoms only started to settle and become more manageable after her diagnosis and following the start of hormone replacement therapy (HRT). She also found that the diagnosis made a huge difference in the workplace. Working for someone who was now able to be empathetic and listen and then tried to find solutions was a huge relief.

Julia's Experience

This section was written by Julia McFarland in her own style:

As I sat at my desk with two fans on full blast (one under my desk to blow up my skirt), I wondered whether I would self-combust. I had also had a period for thirteen days. I couldn't retain any information for longer than five seconds. I wondered if I was losing control of my body and mind.

This was the first time I realised that menopause had stopped me in my tracks. I was so fed up, angry; you name it, I felt it. I was not helped by the fact that, reluctantly, I had shared my feelings and symptoms with my boss, who told me that she had 'sailed through it'. I just needed to take HRT – that apparently would solve all my problems.

My memory grew increasingly unreliable, and I missed a meeting because I had no memory of arranging it. I couldn't cope with what was happening to me and I didn't know how to share my feelings with others. My despair reminded me of when my parents died within four months of each other, and it seemed like the world was coming to an end.

Why couldn't I share these feelings? I think it was because I felt ashamed, embarrassed, and more than a little panic-stricken. It was this embarrassment that inhibited the conversations I needed to have.

After my bereavement, I felt I had a 'legitimate' reason with grief for feeling different. With this change in the state of my health, I didn't. This was something I believed I should be able to cope with, without making a fuss.

The attitude that my boss had expressed is not unique to menopause. I remember my horror when a colleague suffering from severe morning sickness was told that she 'ought to expect it because it was natural.' She was furious that her boss had said to her that she had gone through her pregnancies 'without taking a day off.' Not everyone has the same symptoms and experience with their health. Assumptions that people make are unhelpful and often infuriating.

So, what can you do to work through the change? There are several resources to help you through it, but it's also important to share what is happening with those you need to.

To address my menopause symptoms, I realised that I had to treat it just like my other health condition – asthma. For me, a variety of approaches work to relieve my asthma symptoms, and I recognise and am honest with colleagues when my condition is affecting me. When I began to adopt the same approach with menopause, it helped. Again, this can feel easier said than done, but practice makes perfect.

I realised with the onset of menopause that I needed time to process this change and then practically find solutions that worked for me.

I am writing that last sentence and laughing a bit because it makes it sound easy, and it wasn't. It did take a lot of determination at a time when I was feeling less confident and capable than I normally do. Be kind to yourself and recognise this. Bear in mind the NHS say that symptoms can last from an average of four years to as many as twelve years for one in ten. So that's quite a large variation. Then there are all the symptoms that I haven't mentioned; I counted about thirty-nine. Some of these are difficult to talk about not only with health professionals, but also with partners and family.

The fans are turned off now, and I'm feeling tons better. I remember all my meetings. Make sure that you become part of making your colleagues, family and friends all feel accepted. Help them find practical and factually based advice that prevents them from feeling that the world is coming to an end and that they will never feel the same again. Help them to feel better.

Emily's Experience

Emily summed up the issue in her opening lines when talking to me, 'Every woman goes through menopause, and yet there is no education about it at school.' And there it is: so many women stumble into it without any understanding, and too often take ailments one at a time to a GP only to be prescribed the wrong medication.

In Emily's case, she started having heavy periods after the birth of her daughter, followed by horrible contraction pains when ovulating. She explains it was so bad that for seven years, she couldn't even tie her shoelaces when the pain was coursing through her body. With stomach problems to add to her woes, her GP prescribed IBS treatments. In retrospect, this was not a good idea, and it may have made matters worse.

Emily had a job in the NHS around this time and said that there were no leaflets and no help. She then switched to a line manager who was taking HRT for her menopause, and it set her thinking. The next breakthrough came when she started getting hot flushes and severe mood swings, in addition to stomach cramps and pains. She went to see a new GP, who ordered a batch of blood tests and was finally able to confirm menopause as the root cause of her symptoms.

Emily explains that menopause not only incapacitated her at its monthly peak, but her mood swings led to issues with friends and colleagues, and she would also get brain fog and short-term memory loss accompanying it. The impact was so severe that it led to a need to take a significant amount of time off work and for her doctor to prescribe antidepressants.

One day everything was going wrong. Emily ended up getting into her car, driving too fast down some narrow roads and was tempted to swerve in front of an oncoming bus. She's not sure what held her back, but it was a turning point in her desire to get everything sorted out and, eventually, to start campaigning for a greater understanding of menopause. Looking back, she recognises just how lucky she was to have a daughter who came and spent time with her until she was able to pull through.

Emily remains concerned that even the newly qualified GPs have little training in menopause. And it is serious. Women take their own lives as a consequence of the effects of this life change, and worse still, as a result of being prescribed the wrong HRT treatment on occasion. Relationships suffer as many menopausal women don't want to be touched, are often very tired and lose their libido.

HR Accommodations

Frankie, Julia and Emily suggest the following accommodations:

- Menopause awareness: ensuring that line managers understand the effects of menopause and are open to listening when female employees request help. Frankie works with a predominantly Muslim staff group and understands that some of the male managers find a subject like this difficult to talk about.

- Create menopause mentors: seek volunteers who have been through menopause to provide support and encouragement to those first entering this phase of their life. Simply having someone 'on your side' and listening and empathising from a position of personal understanding can make a huge difference. If the word 'mentor' doesn't work, consider a buddy system for menopausal women to volunteer to be part of and support each other.
- Wellbeing champions: an alternative to menopause mentors for smaller work environments, a wellbeing champion can both provide empathy and support, and help arrange for things like desk fans and changed rotas without it becoming a big issue.
- Create a supervisors' guide for managing menopause.
- MHFA: given that stress and anxiety can accompany menopause, especially amongst those women still trying for a family, it is good to ensure that your mental health first aiders are aware of the side effects of menopause and that they know where to signpost women in their local area.
- Unions and staff reps: some women will feel more comfortable speaking to a staff rep than their line manager or HR. Make sure that the staff reps are as aware of menopause as the line managers.
- Signposting: letting women know about Facebook groups, local support groups, and how to talk to their manager (or HR or GP) can all help enormously in the early stages.
- Flexible working: it's simply not sensible to have people who are suffering from brain fog making key decisions, or for those experiencing big swings in body temperature to be forced to stay at a desk away from an open window. By creating flexibility and allowing choice, you will gain a happier and more productive team.

- Rest room: creating a comfortable area where someone can go for just five or ten minutes to rest, drink some water, recuperate and gather their thoughts can really help.
- Cooling: providing a desk fan can be a life saver. Maybe have a set of fans available for short-term loan from the facilities teams, especially in modern offices where windows can't be opened. Encourage the use of easily removable clothing, like cardigans and jackets.
- One to ones are important to support the colleague in their treatment, and to find out if any changes need to take place. Some people believe that because every woman will go through menopause at some point that they should just 'suck it up'. Treating each person as an individual and understanding that a one-size-fits-all approach won't be applicable can work wonders.
- Get discussions going on things like brain fog and how to deal with it, especially when people are struggling for words in meetings.
- Signpost those women truly suffering from menopause to the specialist practitioners. Emily suggests that a paid consultation with a menopause specialist can lead to reduced time off and increased productivity once the correct therapies have been prescribed.
- Ask facilities to regularly review temperature and humidity ranges in offices where women going through menopause are working, and that the chocolate in the vending machines is regularly replenished!
- As with so many aspects of inclusion, the single biggest things that can help are providing clear means of communication and remembering that everyone is different and affected in different ways. Let's break the taboo! Let's talk about it. Accept that some women are affected by menopause more than others, and allow them space and time to get through it when needed.

Further Resources

www.thebms.org.uk/

www.menopausedoctor.co.uk/

www.menopausesupport.co.uk/

www.themenopausecharity.org/

www.megsmenopause.com/

www.menopausecafe.net/

www.daisynetwork.org/

43

Migraines

A migraine is an intense headache that can be truly debilitating. Unlike a headache, it is normally prominent in one side of the brain. It is sometimes accompanied by changes in vision and smell, auras and nausea, and it can last anywhere from a few hours to several weeks. The NHS states that one in five women regularly suffer from migraines, compared with one in fifteen men. Migraines can be considered a hidden condition because the afflicted person is otherwise outwardly healthy and can go for months without an attack.

Hannah's first migraine happened at the age of eight, when she was returning to school after the weekend. As she looks back over the years, she knows that the main trigger for her is stress: she can eat chocolate, drink caffeinated drinks and withstand all types of smells, which are often the triggers for other people to get a migraine. I asked her to try and explain what the difference is between a headache and a migraine. For her, a headache is a dull pain all over her head, sometimes localised, which can be controlled with over-the-counter medication such as paracetamol.

A migraine for Hannah usually builds from her left or right temple, behind the eye. She becomes light and smell sensitive, her eyes become bloodshot and will try to close due to the light sensitivity, and then she starts to feel nauseous. Meanwhile, her speech becomes confused and she can no longer read the words on a page. Next, she is usually sick and then feels pressure build up in her head and body before she is wiped out by the pain. Others have reported that they get an aura before the migraine or see wiggly lines and spots or even darkness, but Hannah doesn't experience these.

There is no cure for these migraines, and yet there is a range of treatments that work with varying degrees of success for different people. Co-codamol, for example, helps many people, but it does have the side effect of making them feel sick and can cause rebound headaches. Some people are prescribed preventative medications, which are usually used for other conditions, including anti-epilepsy drugs, blood pressure-lowering medicines, anti-anxiety and anti-depression tablets. While Hannah does not take a daily preventative, she uses cooling gel strips, white tiger balms and cold eye masks, as well as applying pressure to the bridge of her nose to ease pain before painkillers take effect. She has tried triptans, but these have proved ineffective for her. The migraine itself normally lasts for six to twelve hours, and Hannah says that sleep really does help; it's just staying asleep is the issue. Lying down in a cold dark room helps.

HR Accommodations

Hannah has been lucky at work, with a caring line manager and an excellent GP. She suggests the following for the workplace:

- Chat to the person about their migraines. If you have never had one, then try to think of a time when you have had the worst-ever hangover, or imagine someone pushing a screwdriver into your head and wiggling it around for several hours, giving you a continuous excruciating sharp, stabbing feeling.
- Can you find them a place in the office to work with good natural lighting? Maybe provide a SAD light source for them, as this is closer to natural lighting and can help reduce the immediate pain.
- Can the IT team provide a high-end monitor with an ultra-fast refresh rate to reduce flicker triggers for those who are sensitive, as well as paying for blue light filters? IT might also be able to look at

inverting their computer screen, which can also help (white text on a black background, as with phones).

- Provide as much flexibility as you can, allowing someone to take a half or full day off if they have an attack or are recovering from one, and make up the time later.
- Make provision in your automated absence recording for people who get migraines. There is no point endlessly asking them to come in for a sickness absence review when their condition means that they cannot work when suffering an attack.

Further Resources
https://www.migrainetrust.org/
https://www.bash.org.uk/

See Also
Blackouts and Hemiplegic Migraine

44

Miscarriage

The loss of an unborn baby understandably brings about many physical and psychological repercussions. All too often this is a hidden issue In the workplace, because women tend not to share news of pregnancy until the second trimester, and they might not yet be emotionally ready to share their family plans with others. Equally, they may not be aware they are pregnant in the first place.

Gemma's first miscarriage occurred on a Friday when she was working at home. The following week she was on annual leave, which meant that she could take time to come to terms with her loss, physically and emotionally, before easing herself back into work just over a week later. On reflection, she thinks this time should have been sick leave, but when it happened, she was in no place to think about that. The return to work was during the Easter holidays, and as Gemma works in education, work was much quieter, which helped. Her second miscarriage happened in the second trimester of pregnancy and was induced following a scan that revealed that the foetus was no longer alive. On this occasion, she needed to take a couple of weeks off work to recover, as well as the week leading up to induction.

As Gemma's first loss was in the first trimester, not many people at work knew she was pregnant; however, she found that when she returned to work, those that did know just didn't know what to say. Some were embarrassed; others tried to avoid social conversations and concentrated on talking about work projects. All Gemma really needed was for someone to sit and listen and ask how she was.

Following Gemma's second loss, the return to work was easier. With Gemma's agreement, her manager had let the team know, and people sent her lovely messages and bought her gifts. Her manager also went out of her way to spend the whole of her first day back in the office with her, helping her catch up with what had been happening and being there to listen when Gemma wanted to talk about her experiences: an act of kindness that she will never forget. Whilst people were still unsure what to say or whether to discuss it, simple comments like 'It's nice to see you back' felt welcoming and as if they acknowledged her absence.

After you have had several miscarriages, and especially when one is late-term, the consultants may elect to check your progress regularly as an outpatient, and even more so when you next become pregnant. Again, Gemma's employers were superb and made flexible arrangements so that she could attend clinics and appointments as and when needed. Gemma had the advantage of being accompanied by her partner, thanks to his workplace being supportive, which helped significantly with reducing the stress and anxiety at each appointment.

Today Gemma has two lovely daughters and volunteers for a charity called Willow's Rainbow Box, which supports families who are pregnant again following loss. The charity has covered topics such as 'Workplace support for pregnancy after loss' in #rainbowbabyhour on Twitter, and they have had many people share their experiences, both good and bad. Gemma also runs an Instagram account, @parenting.after.loss, aimed at promoting positive wellbeing for those who have experienced loss. Through this, many others shared their own experiences of returning to work following miscarriage.

HR Accommodations

Gemma makes the following suggestions for the workplace:

- Try to let the person lead the conversation and explain what support and help they need. Be there just to listen when needed.

- Avoid using phrases like 'At least it happened early on' and, 'When will you be trying again?'. They really do not help.
- Provide as much flexibility as you can for appointments and time off when it is needed.
- Check that your policies include baby loss. It is better that it is explicitly mentioned rather than have to be resolved each time between compassionate leave, sick leave, bereavement leave and holidays.
- Ensure that neither partner rushes back to work; they need to have time to grieve together and be prepared for re-entry into the workplace.
- Do not assume that an early miscarriage is any easier for people to deal with than one later in the pregnancy.
- Accept that the person may exhibit unusually low resilience in the first weeks after return and may have to leave meetings if their emotions are triggered.
- Consider whether their work will involve anything related to pregnancy/babies and discuss making reasonable adjustments with the person if possible.
- Only tell team members and other colleagues when you have the express permission of the person and the agreed wording to use.
- Check that any automated HR absence system reminder emails are put on hold.
- Find ways to talk about miscarriage with MHFAs and in other meetings to help reduce the stigma and educate people on how and why these things happen.

Further Resources

https://www.miscarriageassociation.org.uk/
https://www.tommys.org
https://babyloss-awareness.org/organisations/
http://willowsrainbowbox.co.uk/

See Also
Stillbirth

45

Multiple Sclerosis (MS)

Rosin had a series of different illnesses over a considerable period of time and kept getting told to go home and rest or take analgesic medicines (painkillers) by her doctor. Her symptoms included numbness down her legs, the sensation of pins and needles, a lack of balance, tripping over her own feet, neurological pain, a loss of the ability to discern temperature (hence burning herself by accident) and tiredness. The problem is that MS is difficult to diagnose because it mimics the symptoms of up to twenty other diseases. As a consequence it is not only a hidden condition, but it also hides from doctors.

Rosin kept pressing her doctor to take things seriously. Eventually, she was sent for a series of blood tests and scans and finally a deeply unpleasant lumbar puncture, involving six hours in the hospital followed by the worst headache ever, as her body took time to replace the lost spinal fluid. Thanks to years spent googling her symptoms, the diagnosis of relapsing-remitting MS wasn't a shock in itself, but it took some time to get used to, as Rosin read up and tried to understand what she had and its various effects.

The majority of people with MS have the relapsing-remitting diagnosis which, as the name suggests, means that their symptoms and the severity of the condition, comes and goes over time. Often it is completely hidden, sometimes it is obvious to others. MS is the name given to the breakdown of myelin, the body's protective covering of nerve endings. According to the MS Society it affects around one in five hundred people in the UK and is twice as common in females than males. In addition to the symptoms that Rosin has detailed, others regularly experience blurred vision, loss of bladder control, muscle spasms and memory problems.

Rosin's diagnosis meant that she now knew what she was tackling, and she entered the next stage in her life, deciding to go down the disease-modifying treatment route. At one point this resulted in taking up to thirty-seven pills a day plus injections, to both control the MS and the side effects of the MS drugs.

Currently, there is no cure for MS, albeit there are disease-modifying therapies that have been in use for about five years, which slow progression down. Most of the medicines simply reduce the impact of the symptoms. As an example, one of the medicines that Rosin was prescribed in the past is a beta interferon. This was injected with a pen at home and aimed to help reduce the inflammation that damages the nerve endings in her body when the MS flared up. It needed to be kept refrigerated. Although that particular therapy did not work for Rosin, who has since moved to a once-a-day tablet that is much easier to manage, it has been effective for many other people.

Of all the many symptoms, the one that Rosin fears most is the possibility that she could wake up to discover that she can no longer see. The mere knowledge that this is a possibility can lead to anxiety, and in turn, depression, both of which can result in the MS worsening, a vicious cycle if intervention does not occur. Other issues that can lead to a worsening are tiredness, hot temperatures, bad weather and mistakes with her diet.

The pandemic has not helped. Rosin is clinically vulnerable due to the use of the immunosuppressant drugs she is taking, meaning she is liable to catch anything doing the rounds. Public transport and even trips to the local shops are no-go areas when it is flu season, let alone Covid. One person's sniffle is Rosin's major chest infection, with all the complications that brings.

Rosin says the most difficult aspect in the work setting is that MS is unpredictable, variously affecting her hearing, sight, balance, smell and taste, as well as giving her brain fog. Occasionally she will get a flare-up, often triggered by stress, meaning that things like restructuring at work need to be carefully thought through. Flare-ups damage her spinal cord with varying results, but could, in a worst-case scenario, leave her in a wheelchair. More likely, she would have to recover in bed for several days.

Even though she has to live with MS every day of her life and never knows what she will be waking up to, Rosin is one of those amazing people who still lives life to the full. She's a futurist with a passion for change, she's a volunteer coach and mentor, and she managed to make me laugh during what could have been an exceptionally sombre discussion about her condition.

HR Accommodations

Rosin's tips for the workplace include:

- Read up and understand as much as you can about MS.
- Allow plenty of scope for truly flexible working. There will be days where your colleague needs rest and other days when they will be working full-on. Furthermore, they will need to attend outpatient clinics for quarterly blood tests and six-monthly scans.
- Actively think about stress management when change is planned. Take your colleague into confidence before major announcements. For example, explain that restructuring is going to be announced and what the actual consequences will be. Don't leave it vague or uncertain, thereby causing anxiety or stress.
- When stressful situations arise at work (change in management, restructure, merger etc), offer extra counselling, coaching or mentoring.
- If your MS colleague is about to join a new team or a project, talk to them about how to let other colleagues know about MS and how best to provide support. Be led by them.

- When people understand what it means to have MS, they can be more supportive and inclusive. At its very simplest level, they need to understand that they cannot catch it.
- Provide a space where your MS colleague can self-inject medications (a toilet cubicle is neither pleasant nor conducive) and a fridge space to keep medicines cool, preferably without either being obvious to everyone else.
- If you provide health and life insurance, disclose the diagnosis to your provider. Do not discriminate against them by reducing cover levels.
- If travel for work is essential, talk to your colleague about how best to make arrangements and, if they are going abroad, make sure that adequate insurance and provision for refrigeration of medication (for example, in the hotel and on the plane) is provided.
- Ensure that you have up-to-date next of kin/partner details, as well as their GP or consultant's details, just in case there is a flare-up at work.
- Make provision for them to be able to work at home; this will be particularly helpful on outpatient days or when there is a bug going around work.
- MS drugs prescribed by hospitals are considered 'controlled' drugs and tend not to be available through regular pharmacies, as they are expensive to stock and will only help a limited number of customers. Deliveries are set up monthly with companies like Healthcare at Home, who have to deliver to the individual or a named person on an agreed date. For this reason, allowing individuals to accept deliveries at work can be incredibly helpful.

Further Resources

https://www.mssociety.org.uk/
https://mstrust.org.uk/

https://www.thebraincharity.org.uk/how-we-can-help/practical-help/information-advice/a-z-of-conditions/44-m/194-multiple-sclerosis

46

Obsessive-Compulsive Disorder (OCD) and Scrupulosity OCD

OCD is a mental health condition, or anxiety disorder, that affects about one per cent of the population, the majority of whom are younger women. It is a broad term that covers elements of repetitive or repeating behaviour, emotions, desires and compulsions to do things, many of which others believe are unnecessary or irrational. It can range from someone suffering from unwanted (often nasty) thoughts continually entering their head to a need to check and recheck that a door has been locked, or to always have to turn a switch on and off a set number of times. OCD is hidden, but it can affect productivity and it can become debilitating in extreme cases.

Anne's Experience

Anne has just realised that she was driving at 33mph in an area with a limit of 30mph. She has a mild panic. She looks for police cars, cameras, signs of anyone who might have witnessed her. She pulls over and checks on the internet for the allowable margin of error. Google suggests ten per cent. Her speed of 33mph might just be okay. She phones her best friend to ask. She seeks assurance. She rings off. She thinks about going to the police station to voluntarily report her misdemeanour. She phones her friend again, just to check. She heads home and worries about it for several months until she is satisfied that a summons won't drop on her doorstep.

Everyone goes through an event like this every so often, but for Anne, it might happen several times a day. Unlike some people who have OCD, she doesn't compulsively clean her house, have rituals associated with leaving the house (such as checking and rechecking the windows), keep everything in orderly patterns, nor is she hyper-organised. But she does have a need to know exactly where the boundary between right and wrong exists, and she ensures that everything is black or white; grey is problematic.

OCD for Anne also comes in the form of intrusive thoughts, which are far from pleasant. She starts to think she is a bad person or that she has been abrasive or unkind, and again needs to seek reassurance. She may even have a fleeting thought about undertaking a bad act, such as pouring boiling water over someone's foot, but thankfully those thoughts never translate into action. Again, such random thoughts are not uncommon, but it's the frequency with which Anne has to live with such thoughts and their 'getting stuck' in her consciousness that define her condition.

In the work environment, Anne likes to know the set rules and regulations and then wants to ensure that they are operated to the letter. Situations where there are rules that nobody follows make her feel uncomfortable, knowing that not following them is wrong. She often feels guilty. Although it might seem trivial, a small thing such as using company Post-it notes for a personal matter might mean worrying about using company equipment for the wrong purpose and then buying a new pack on the way to work the next day to replace it. Anne is surprisingly rational about her condition; she lives with the knowledge, for example, that she can coach others in how to make decisions in the grey zone – she just can't resolve them for herself.

Anne lived with her OCD, knowing nothing different from her early years, but it was when it started to impact both her working *and* private life that she realised she needed help. She undertook weekly counselling with a trained therapist and learned CBT (Cognitive Behavioural Therapy) techniques. Her first priority was to manage her anxiety, to bring the levels down so that she could access logical thinking and use one of the techniques for dealing with the 'intrusion'. Today she regularly uses guided meditation and mindfulness to keep her life in balance.

Now that she has learned a set of techniques and that she has a therapist she can call when needed, Anne has a healthy level of control back over her life and is therefore looking at how she can support others. If you can provide the appropriate support, you will be rewarded, especially if the people that you meet are anything like as bright and intelligent and positive as Anne.

Ellie's Experience

OCD is not, in Ellie's case, about being obsessively clean and tidy or about having everything arranged in alphabetical order on the bookcase. She doesn't have to recheck that the taps are turned off and windows are shut before she goes on holiday (the compulsive part of OCD). Instead, Ellie gets intrusive thoughts, one of the more difficult forms of the obsessive part of OCD to try and support.

Ellie remembers her childhood as being a time when she had a wild imagination, but it was also a time of sorrow, with some sad experiences of facing the death of loved ones. As she grew older, her imagination grew more intense and stayed with her for many more hours at a time. Intrusive thoughts can come into her head at any time of the day or night; she has no control over them. Once they are there, she often needs to act upon them, and it is frequently exhausting.

By way of example, Ellie explains that she is constantly thinking about her father. When he tells her he is going to the pub, she starts planning to be there when he leaves because she is concerned that he might be mugged on the way home or suffer a heart attack.

Ellie lives in the top apartment with her two cats and a dog. When her partner has a shower and leaves the window open to air the bathroom, Ellie has to go in and close it, fearing that one of the cats might fall out to its death. In other words, she catastrophises.

Ellie explains that she needs to be in control to ensure the safety of everyone close to her. She believes that if she doesn't take action, then something bad might happen. Once those thoughts are in her head, they don't leave quickly, and often she will get little sleep as a consequence.

When Ellie was diagnosed with OCD, her GP referred her for CBT (cognitive behavioural therapy). She has tried this twice now but to no avail. There is no cure. Some people are prescribed medicines, known as SSRIs (selective serotonin reuptake inhibitors), but they can take a long time to take effect, and they can have other unwanted side effects.

Regarding work, Ellie needs flexible working hours and an understanding manager. She needs to be able to phone in and explain that she has had no sleep, that she can barely open her eyes, and will catch up later. Ideally, she needs a flexible part-time role, but these are few and far between. Working from home gives her more flexibility, so the changes aligned with Covid may well give her an unexpected benefit in time, but Ellie is wary of declaring her condition in the application process, fearing that she will not be employed once they know about her condition.

HR Accommodations

Anne and Ellie suggest the following accommodations for the workplace:

- When someone discloses that they are diagnosed with OCD, invite them to chat privately with you. Ask them to tell you about their condition, how it affects them and the support mechanisms that they use. Everyone has a different experience and different symptoms, so forget anything that you think you know and listen. There are many different types of OCD, and the help and support one individual might appreciate can be vastly different from another, even if they have the same 'type' of OCD.
- Ask the person how you and the organisation can best help them, when you should intervene, signs to look for, etc.

- Be ready to provide support if the person has an issue with the interpretation of rules and procedures, or gets stuck checking something once too often.
- Prepare to provide more reassurance than you would normally expect to have to give.
- If your organisation expects people to regularly work in different areas (e.g. hot-desking), consider whether a fixed desk for a person with OCD might be more productive.
- Check that they are getting the appropriate therapeutic counselling support. If they have just been diagnosed and are waiting a long time for NHS provision, consider paying privately as an organisation. The increase in productivity will repay the costs quickly.
- Allow time off for clinic and counselling appointments, and provide flexible working to allow the person to take time out when needed.

Further Resources

https://www.ocduk.org/

https://www.mind.org.uk/information-support/types-of-mental-health-problems/obsessive-compulsive-disorder-ocd/about-ocd/

https://iocdf.org/about-ocd/who-gets/

https://ocdaction.org.uk/wp-content/uploads/2019/12/employing_people_with_ocd_0916_1.pdf

Obsessive-Compulsive Disorder: The Facts by Padmal De Silva

47

Panic Attacks

'My body starts overheating. My head feels like it's exploding. I can clearly hear my heartbeat inside my head. All logical thinking ceases. My chest tightens. I can't breathe. I can't hear anything. I collapse to the ground. I turn grey as all the colour drains from my face.'

It was at this point that Simon's manager thought he was having a heart attack and called for an ambulance. The paramedics arrived, checked his heart and recognised the signs of a panic attack, then helped Simon stabilise himself. When he started to feel sick, the crew knew he was on the mend.

A panic attack is accompanied by a huge dose of adrenalin that surges through the body. It is related to the fight or flight mechanism that early man needed to be able to survive when being attacked by wild animals or facing a fire. In Simon's case, his body overproduced the adrenaline, causing his body to collapse.

When Simon is about to give a presentation at work or attend a meeting that he knows might be stressful, he has now learned to carry out some simple breathing and mindfulness exercises beforehand, to drink soothing herbal remedies and prepare himself as best he can. On occasions, though, a panic attack comes from nowhere, even when he is in a safe environment with no pressure. It is this latter situation that means he has to alert new line managers and colleagues, just in case it happens again. He wants to avoid someone trying to stimulate his heart with a resuscitation technique!

Simon, who is outwardly healthy, has had several conversations with doctors about his panic attacks. Some have offered medicines, such as antidepressants and benzodiazepines. Unless it is taken over an extended period of time, no medicine can act fast enough to prevent a panic attack, and many have side effects that are either addictive or dull other senses; hence Simon has looked for alternatives. He uses apps on his phone like Calm, and utilises many of the free resources available on the Headspace and MIND websites.

HR Accommodations:

If a colleague discloses that they are prone to panic attacks, then think about the following:

- Check that it is okay to tell others in the workplace and educate people on what a panic attack is, what it can look like, and how to help if it happens. Tell first aiders and MHFAs in confidence, with the employee's permission.
- If a major change is about to occur at work, take the person to one side and privately brief them on what is happening so that they are not suddenly exposed to an event in an environment that they can't control. For example, don't announce a redundancy programme in front of a large group without confidentially warning your colleague first.
- Provide easy-to-access resources (many are free) on your intranet that covers all aspects of mental health and, in particular, recognise that everyone can suffer an occasional panic attack or anxiety attack.
- Check that your organisation's EAR service includes counselling opportunities for people facing additional stress or anxiety. This can be particularly helpful during a restructure, merger or similar. Paying a small amount more for additional external support can be invaluable.

Further Resources

https://www.mind.org.uk/information-support/types-of-mental-health-problems/anxiety-and-panic-attacks/panic-attacks/

https://www.calm.com/

https://www.headspace.com/

48

Phobias

Phobias – typically, a fear of something or of a situation – affect the majority of the population in a mild form. The most common phobias include:

- Acrophobia (heights)
- Agoraphobia (open spaces)
- Arachnophobia (spiders)
- Astraphobia (thunder and lightning)
- Claustrophobia (confined spaces)
- Cynophobia (dogs)
- Emetophobia (vomit)
- Glossophobia (public speaking)
- Mysophobia (germs or dirt)
- Ophidiophobia (snakes)
- Pteromerhanophobia or Aerophobia (flying)
- Social Phobia (fear of social gatherings and parties)
- Trypanophobia (injections)

Symptoms of a phobia are anxiety and panic when coming into contact with the cause. With the possible exception of the fears of snakes, dogs and injections, most of these phobias can be triggered in the workplace. Whilst for most people phobias are mild, some can be quite intense and can hold a person back from progression in their career, and consequently, a reduction in productivity. Fear of public speaking is the most obvious, but other phobias can play a part as well.

For example, I discovered that a member of my team would never come and eat in the canteen because she was concerned that either she would be sick or someone else would be sick. She used to explain that she preferred to eat her packed lunch in the park near the offices so that she could get out of the building. In doing so, she missed out on social bonding and knowledge of what was happening in the organisation.

Another team member never volunteered to undertake projects abroad because of his fear of flying, his excuse being that he couldn't leave his family at that time. He missed out on some significant development opportunities and promotions. If only I had known earlier.

One consultant I partnered with would always tell me how she liked climbing stairs to keep fit. It was only later that she explained that she couldn't use lifts or stay for too long in a small office because of her fear of small spaces. Quite an issue when visiting a client halfway up the Canary Wharf building, albeit their conference room was huge!

As exemplified above, most people do not talk about their phobias; they don't want to be belittled or teased by others. When they do, it is important to take the matter seriously and help them find appropriate support. Treatments for phobias include talking therapies, such as cognitive behavioural therapy and sometimes medicines.

Simple phobias can be treated through gradual exposure to the object, animal, place or situation that causes fear and anxiety. This is known as desensitisation or self-exposure therapy. To succeed, they are best run with the help of a professional or as part of a self-help programme.

Treating complex phobias may involve a combination of cognitive behavioural therapy, psychotherapy, counselling and rarely a medication such as antidepressants, tranquillisers or beta blockers. Hypnosis can be helpful too, in the same way that it can be used to form new mental pathways and stop bad habits like smoking. Therapy discussions focus on the understanding that nobody is born with a phobia and trying to understand what triggered the phobia (often an event in childhood). Seeing the phobia for what it is and ensuring that one bad experience shouldn't be mapped across all experiences often helps unlock the phobia.

HR Accommodations

- A colleague talking about their phobia is a special moment. Listen and try to understand how it affects them. You are not an expert in this field. Suggest they seek a referral from their GP, or arrange for them to discuss the issues with your Occupational Health provider or a trained counsellor.
- Do not attempt therapy (e.g. forcing them to fly); leave this to the trained professionals.
- Provide appropriate support so that they don't miss out. Update them with details of what happened at an event they missed; offer to buddy with them whilst treatment progresses.

Further Resources

https://www.anxietyuk.org.uk/anxiety-type/phobias/

https://www.mind.org.uk/information-support/types-of-mental-health-problems/phobias/about-phobias/

https://www.topuk.org/

49

Polycystic Ovary Syndrome
(PCOS)

At least one in four women experience the effects of Polycystic Ovary Syndrome to differing degrees, with one in ten being significantly affected. The condition has a confusing name. Although it suggests that the ovaries grow cysts, they actually develop fluid-filled sacs, called follicles, around the eggs and the ovaries enlarge. In most cases, the ovaries develop many small follicles and fail to release eggs on a regular basis. It is not yet understood why this happens; research continues. PCOS is a genetic condition. Symptoms include weight gain, oily skin, adult acne, excessive hair growth on the body and/or hair loss on the head and face, physical pain, poor sleep, irregular or no periods and difficulty becoming pregnant. Some people can also experience diabetes, headaches, high blood pressure, cholesterol imbalance and sleep apnoea.

Alejandra's Experience
Alejandra had just turned twenty when she started to research her irregular periods. Having gone for five months without her cycle and knowing that she wasn't pregnant, she raised it with her GP, and after a series of tests and scans, learned that she had PCOS. In retrospect, she is pleased that she took it seriously; she has since learned that without treatment, she may have become infertile. Her desire is that more women should be made aware of the condition. The upside to this chapter is that she has two healthy little girls running around her house.

Some people require surgery to remove or burst the follicles whilst, in Alejandra's case, she was placed on a combined oestrogen and progesterone pill to rebalance her hormone system and encourage the eggs to be released at normal intervals. Her menstrual cycle was extremely heavy, and she also required magnesium supplements to help her body due to blood loss. There were many accidents at work due to this; on one occasion, she had to go home early from work, as the bleeding had permeated all the layers of her clothes and there was no way that she could continue to work.

In the work environment, Alejandra is amazed at how few people know about the condition and its effects. And worse, she is concerned about how few make an effort to understand or show any empathy, passing it off as just something you have to live with. And yet, it is not only painful but can be debilitating when the period does come, being so heavy and requiring regular attention. Alejandra explains that she suffers headaches, fatigue and nausea, has zero motivation to do anything, and is wiped out by the large loss of blood. If menstruation starts during the working week, she either has to get an agreement to work from home (not easy, pre-pandemic), take a holiday, or risk being put on review for having a regular pattern of sick days.

Alejandra was already on the trigger sickness absence policy due to the number of days that she had taken due to her condition, and was even called to an informal sickness meeting to discuss her absences. She says that since having her daughters, her periods have become much lighter, and she can now socialise and not go through the pain that she used to beforehand.

Sofia's Experience

Sofia had her first menstrual cycle when she was fourteen, but rather than a regular monthly event, they were sporadic and random. At sixteen, her GP said that she was young, her body was just settling down and she shouldn't be concerned, so she got on with life and became a professional athlete, living with her odd cycles.

In her late teens, Sofia stopped her training and decided to go on the combined contraceptive pill to help regulate her cycles. Later, in her twenties, she decided to give her body a break from the hormones and came off the pill, which she had been on for about eight years. She rapidly put on weight, even though her diet was the same. She knew that it wasn't right, and so she went to see her GP, who this time ordered blood tests.

The results showed that Sofia had higher levels of androgens (testosterone in particular) and insulin in her body than was normal, consistent with PCOS. In essence, her hormone system was out of kilter and needed correction. For her, the impact was weight gain and irregular periods, with anxiety and phases of depression.

Having been diagnosed, Sofia researched PCOS and learned that it was linked to her metabolism, hence the weight gain, and also to the production of insulin. Sofia had no desire to have children, but she noted that infertility was a common side effect. At first, Sofia was treated with metformin, but it had no effect, and the only other alternative treatment was to go back on the combined hormonal contraceptive pill, which she opted not to do due to the side effects and risks that come with this approach. In 2015 she had the cysts on her ovaries removed by surgery, which helped reduce the androgen levels, and then worked hard on her diet, alongside a full exercise programme. Part of the generic advice given is that she should avoid stress – not easy in any job these days!

HR Accommodations

Alejandra and Sofia suggest that HR teams could help with the following:

- Agreeing to a flexible work schedule. Understand that when an irregular menstrual cycle arrives, it may well be heavy and tiring, and the person may need time off work to rest and recover. This also applies to morning cramps, which might make it hard for someone to get out of bed first thing, needing to wait until they can move.

- Being aware that cramping can occur throughout the day. Working from home would be a good option to review due also to the heaviness of these period cycles.

- Being sensitive about maternity leave, celebration events, baby photos, etc. It could be that this person really wants children but can't have them.

- Providing sensitivity training to all line managers about the range of hidden conditions that people can have and how to handle them in a reasonable way, especially not to leap the conclusion that someone is slacking or not taking their job seriously if they are late or need to take sick days. 'Women's problems' is not an excuse and can be seriously debilitating for some.

- Considering the appointment of wellbeing managers or champions to be available for discussions that might be too difficult to hold with a line manager.

- PCOS can lead to infertility and make the person more susceptible to other conditions, so please listen carefully and read up about the condition to fully understand it.

- Making adjustments to your sickness absence policy to allow for people with PCOS (and other diagnosed long-term conditions) to take breaks when needed and to attend clinics.

- Provide emotional support, empathy, understanding and possibly counselling where the woman is affected by infertility, which is often associated with PCOS.

Further Resources

https://www.verity-pcos.org.uk/
https://www.pcosaa.org/

50

Post-Traumatic Stress Disorder (PTSD)

When most people hear the terms 'Post Traumatic Stress Disorder' or 'PTSD', they immediately think of troops who have returned from an active battlefield. But most people who are suffering from the effects of trauma have never been near a battlefield. In Tim's case, he walked into a house where he found his friend hanging over the staircase. Being a first responder to suicide is grim. To this day, he can't remember the detail of what he saw. Tim tried to bury his experience; something that he has since learned made his PTSD far worse than if he had faced it, accepted early counselling and talked it through regularly with others.

Suicide leaves a huge impact on many people. Everyone wonders if they could have done more to prevent the event, but when you are the first responder, you may also have a memory that will never fully go away. For Tim, this was made worse by the knowledge that he'd previously saved lives both as a lifeguard and as a security guard when he was the person that a suicidal individual reached out to. This background made his PTSD even more complex: he'd saved the lives of complete strangers yet had failed to save his closest friend.

Many forms of trauma can trigger PTSD. Tim's experience is at the extreme end, but many are diagnosed following the break-up of a marriage, a messy redundancy process, abuse, rape or another life-changing event. Tim found in the first four weeks after the event that he became devoid of emotion, and he changed from being a peaceful, quietly spoken person into a new character who was volatile, terse and prone to violent outbursts. At four weeks, the enormity of what had happened hit him hard, and he was referred to a counsellor.

Tim remembers very little about the first counselling session. Everything was a blur. He left the offices and walked straight out in front of traffic, narrowly avoiding a nasty accident. He hadn't been advised properly; he should have attended that first session with a friend or family member.

Tim had excellent support at work. His HR manager worked alongside occupational health to get him the support he needed. He met a psychologist who had himself been a first responder to a friend's suicide, so his empathy and first-hand knowledge were genuine. Tim undertook weekly counselling and CBT (cognitive behavioural therapy) sessions, took appropriate medicines and received support from friends and colleagues. His employer has subsequently expanded OH to include counselling, so not only is the employee physically able to return to work, but also in a position mentally to do so.

Tim explains that the medicines are key to his treatment; they keep him at a decent baseline so that his CBT and counselling can have a positive effect. The meds take a while to get used to and to find the right dosage level, which is different for everyone. Whilst he originally started on opiates and benzodiazepine, he has now moved on to simpler antidepressants, a sign that the therapeutic pathway is slowly succeeding, but this is now more than seven years since the event, showing just how long treatment can take.

Tim is still a changed person. He remembers that prior to the incident that he was famed for how he could handle angry customers at work. Now, he has to avoid such circumstances for fear of setting off his anxiety, which is always just below the surface. He used to sit and listen to people giving their excuses. Now he says he can't tolerate BS; maybe there is at least one upside to balance the downsides.

Some people suffer flashbacks to the event triggered by pictures, smells, anniversary dates, news or social media channels. Always be aware that the anxiety can flare up again on such occasions.

HR Accommodations

Tim suggests the following accommodations in the workplace:

- Everyone handles trauma in a different way. Just because someone doesn't express it through tears and requests for time off, do not assume they are fine. A steely exterior can be hiding a messed-up mind. Take time to listen to the person, refer them to occupational health or encourage them to return to their GP as appropriate.
- Show compassion, empathy and provide a genuinely open door, responding fast when you get a call, text or email about their condition. Remember they have experienced something so far out of the ordinary that you will struggle to get close to understanding from your own frame of reference.
- Allow flexible working as the person starts on their recovery path. Accept that there may be days when they will struggle to even get up in the morning.
- Give paid time off to attend consultant or GP appointments; offer support as needed.
- Encourage them to use counselling services. Don't expect them to return straight to work after a session; the counselling itself can be upsetting and emotionally draining at times.
- Consider a phased return to work, maybe meeting them beforehand to brief them on what has happened and to agree on what work colleagues should know.
- Give whatever help you can if the person needs to move house. A traumatic event in the home sometimes requires a physical relocation to give the mind the chance to recover.

Further Resources

https://www.ptsduk.org/

https://www.mind.org.uk/information-support/types-of-mental-health-problems/post-traumatic-stress-disorder-ptsd-and-complex-ptsd/symptoms/

https://www.thebraincharity.org.uk/how-we-can-help/practical-help/information-advice/a-z-of-conditions/47-p/630-post-traumatic-stress-disorder

51

Prostate Cancer

Nikau was in his mid-fifties when he started to need to pee more often than normal, especially at night. He thought nothing of it; he was well aware that things like this happened as you got older. Time passed, and he started to get pain when urinating – he describes it as a continuous burning sensation. He thought he might have a urinary infection, and so he finally booked an appointment with his doctor. He admits that he delayed the appointment by four days because he wanted to see a male doctor rather than a female.

The morning of the appointment, things had worsened: he noticed a discolouration in his urine, possibly blood. He went to the meeting fearful of the result. The doctor was thorough, and carried out an uncomfortable rectal exam. He said that it felt like his prostate was enlarged and that for safety, it would be best to run some blood tests. Nikau took a printout from the surgery receptionist with him straight to his local outpatients' phlebotomy clinic and gave samples of both blood and urine to be tested.

His fears were well-founded. Just a couple of days later, his doctor called him to say he would need to attend for a scan because the PSA test (prostate-specific antigen) had been positive, and the doctor needed to know if there was a cancerous lump in the area that was causing the pain. By now, Nikau was reading every website and starting to think about writing a will. He was worried that he hadn't acted soon enough and that it might now be too late. He had some sleepless nights and knew that he was a bit short with people in the office.

The scan found a lump in addition to evidence of an enlarged prostate, and that led to a decision to undertake a biopsy of the lump. Nikau was placed under a care team, who surprised him by saying that the results of the biopsy and the scans were such that they didn't want to opt for radical surgery at this stage, which itself might have side effects, and chose to keep him under regular surveillance. In practice, this meant three monthly outpatient returns for blood tests and scans.

About fifteen months later, he was called in to see a consultant and had what he describes as the worst conversation of his life. The lump had grown, and there was a danger of it spreading if not removed. Surgery followed a couple of weeks later, followed by direct radiotherapy into one small area. He lived through a lengthy period of pain, constantly moving and trying to reposition himself, whether sitting down or lying, he leaked urine and had to wear adult nappies, and he kept getting random intense headaches (something he had never suffered from before). Without surgery and radiotherapy there was a real possibility that the cancer would spread to his other organs, and lead to his premature death.

The good news? That was twelve years ago, and since then, he has had regular outpatient visits, but all have been fine. He keeps to a recommended diet and drinks far more water than he ever dreamt possible (he used to smile at the people bringing their water bottles to work, now he is one of them). He has been advised to always get the latest flu jab and was prioritised for Covid vaccination.

Nikau says that he confided in his (female) HR Manager at work at the time that he had to go into hospital. She promised to keep it confidential, and he was pleased that his line manager had only ever asked how he was and no details. Aside from the medical care team, who were great at answering questions, he used the EAR service that his company paid for and received some counselling that he felt had been good for his mental health. He downplayed the need for people to treat this as anything but an issue of ill health that required diagnosis and resolution. Nikau had subsequently met other people with prostate cancer on a Facebook page, who said they had been diagnosed as a consequence of annual employee health checks. In retrospect, his only wish was that he had been tested earlier.

HR Accommodations
Nikau's thoughts for the work environment are as follows:

- If someone talks to you about prostate cancer, remember that for many, it is an intensely private matter. It can affect their sexual health, and therefore they may want absolute confidentiality, unlike other conditions where people are happy to chat in the office about them. Listen and try to be as flexible as you can in your support, especially around needs for time off for clinics and any surgery.
- Consider offering a PSA test to all men on an annual basis in the same way that some companies are now providing regular mammograms via travelling clinics (a clinic in a lorry attends the workplace and tests all who want to take part). If prostate cancer is diagnosed early, then treatment can be much simpler.
- Be careful not to apply sick pay limits when someone has to take a day every two weeks for a clinic, such as radiotherapy. They are not skiving; their need is genuine and must be supported.
- Consider providing additional counselling support to someone with cancer. This is not something that the NHS has the capacity for, and your EAR scheme may not provide sufficient expert coverage.

Further Resources
https://prostatecanceruk.org/
https://tackleprostate.org/
https://orchid-cancer.org.uk/about-us/

See Also

Breast Cancer

Hodgkin Lymphoma

52

Rejection Sensitive Dysphoria (RSD)

For many people, the fear of being disliked determines the actions they take: they accept projects they would rather not do; they attend an event they would prefer to miss; they don't speak out against a colleague; they volunteer to do something they dislike; they work many extra hours without compensation, and even more seriously, they allow themselves to be bullied or abused. You will hear some people say they don't care what others think. They are often the ones that care the most.

Being liked and being a part of society has deep roots. As cave dwellers, humans lived in groups to protect each other from the elements and predators, in the same way that wild animals live in herds or packs. Being rejected by a group in most human society is therefore hurtful and distressing at a deep level.

At its most simple level, most people are concerned with being liked at one point or another. So many of us wish we didn't care what others think, and yet it's virtually impossible not to care at least a little bit. And if we don't care at all, that leads to other social problems.

Rejection Sensitive Dysphoria (RSD) applies to that group of people who are far more sensitive to the possibility of rejection than others, and who perceive that they are being rejected more often than they actually are. They detect a hint of criticism, or the possibility of a negative judgement, never intended by the other party, and overreact to it. An example might include being accidentally missed from an email chain or a team diary invite and assuming it was deliberate.

Reactions can range from physical illness to mental strife: in some cases, rage, and in others, an overcompensation to try to win their place back. In talking about the matter with others, they might exaggerate how people are set against them or how much people dislike them. It can lead to others judging them as being too reactive, hypersensitive or inappropriately perfectionist.

Outside of work, people with RSD can find relationships difficult to maintain, even within their family. They will read far more than is normal into situations because they focus on small details that they perceive are not working out right. For example, a slight delay when asking a partner's opinion on their outfit can lead to the assumption that their partner was trying to conjure a polite response, and they will change their clothes as a consequence. The frequent need to seek assurance about a romantic liaison can itself lead to the ending of the engagement by the partner.

Treatment for RSD is part dependent on the comorbidities (other conditions) that the person has to live with and its severity. Many are on the autism or ADHD spectrum and may well already be receiving medication (including those used to treat depression and high blood pressure) or psychological support (including cognitive behavioural therapy) for that.

Psychotherapies focus on improving understanding of emotional reactions and learning more appropriate responses. Finding ways to control and invalidate dysfunctional thoughts that make the person believe they have been rejected are also key. Cognitive Behavioural Therapy, Dialectical Behaviour Therapy, Acceptance and Commitment Therapy can all be employed to good effect.

I had the opportunity to talk to Roberto about his experiences. When Roberto was a young boy, he thought he could become anything or nothing. He was rebellious and naughty. He left school at sixteen after failing half his exams and went off the rails: caravans, motorbikes, drink and drugs became his life. A job as a plumbing and heating engineer kept him fed and watered. When Roberto was twenty-five, his mum, who was dying from cancer, asked him what he planned to do with his life. Knowing that he was bright, she encouraged him to take a degree. He chose construction management, and he found a job in the field soon after graduating. This led to a series of progressively more critical and demanding roles in the industry, eventually specialising in large-scale project management.

Roberto realised early on that he was different to most people he knew. He was capable of solving immensely complex problems; it's just that he wasn't always listened to and struggled to get his view across. He could throw a wild temper and lived life on a very short fuse. He was seen as lacking in compassion and empathy. He was blunt, and some called him caustic.

Fast forward to 2010, when Roberto applied for a senior promotion at the engineering consultancy where he had worked for nine years. The interview process was tough; he excelled and got some of the highest scores in the analytical and cognitive sections, but was deemed to have low emotional intelligence and was rejected as a consequence. This was a big blow to Roberto. He became depressed and was eventually referred to an occupational psychologist. In retrospect, it might have helped him understand the promotion situation if he had been guided to understand himself many years earlier.

Following the occupational psychologist session, Roberto was referred to a psychiatrist to help treat his long-term depression. Luckily for him, the psychiatrist was also an expert in diagnosing and treating adult ADHD (Attention Deficit Hyperactivity Disorder). He was diagnosed with ADHD with comorbid Asperger's and RSD. He was helped to understand his condition, and how to make adjustments, how to start living a new life with it. Roberto feels strongly that ADHD should be ADHC; it is not a disorder, rather it is a condition. He also argues that ADHD is too big a catch-all. He, for example, says that he doesn't have attention deficits, and he is well aware that he struggles with rejection.

Dysphoria has Greek origins. Loosely translated, it means 'difficult to bear' and is used to infer a state of dissatisfaction, unhappiness, frustration or restlessness. When a person suffers from RSD, they can feel strong emotions and even pain due to being rejected or criticised or by failing to meet the standards that they think have been set for them. Often this is a misperception, but for them, it feels authentic and leads to anxiety and depression until it is either explained or rationalised.

When Roberto 'came out' with his ADHD and RSD diagnosis at work, he found that people didn't know how to react. All they could see in front of them was a physically able, competent engineer: yet inside that physical incarnation, a complex series of processes made him appear to be rude to some, lacking self-discipline and impulsive to others, at best an odd character. Being open about his condition meant he could start to be himself at work and reduce the amount of stage make-up that he had to apply before going to work each day (an excellent analogy for the daily fight that many people have trying to hide a condition).

Roberto's long-term partner describes him as full of energy and drive, with an enthusiasm for life that never stops. She has witnessed his darker side and uses code words to rebalance when he starts to say things that might be hurtful or surprising to others. She also has to work hard to compensate for the things that he is not good at, like building new social relationships, maintaining friendships and sorting out his admin.

Roberto has identified that he needs meaningful goals, the space to work the problem and find his own way around it and regular positive affirmation that all is well. Pay and bonuses don't motivate him; he is not materialistic, but he does crave thanks and positive support. Indeed, he would trade public praise for cash any day.

So what does happen when Roberto gets faint praise, a dressing down, or worst of all, a request to re-do a piece of work? He explains that the rejection hits him fast. His face goes white as the blood drains out, and he tries to find a way out of the room quickly. On one occasion, he collapsed with the shock and was left looking like he had suffered from a stroke. Rejection in people with RSD can manifest itself as a physical change in their body. Alternatives to this more physical reaction range from apologising profusely to swearing and shouting profanities. He has to try extremely hard to control these initial responses and often has to apologise later or explain himself when called to a meeting with the HR team. Controlling emotions is often made more difficult if he feels trapped, cornered or the person giving negative feedback persists. People with RSD, like Roberto, are quick to get the point, and so repetition only serves to make their reaction stronger.

One of the added complications for Roberto is that hierarchy means nothing to him. He is equally at home chatting to the apprentice as he is to the CEO. He works hard to be friends with everyone he meets and will often hear the things that they are interested in and play to them. He craves feeling wanted, and he believes that trust is critical. He is prepared to give trust until it is broken, and at that point, few people can return to his fold. This can mean that he has issues with his bosses at work. With no regard for titles, and a desire to be friends, he finds that it is far too easy to cross the line and then be accused of intruding on their personal space. For example, Roberto struggles with the phrase 'it's not appropriate'. Indeed, he has learned to be somewhat cold to females in the workplace, just in case his attempts to make friendships are misinterpreted. And 'keep your emotions to yourself' is impossible. End of!

Having met Roberto on several occasions, all I can say is that he is a remarkable man and one that is well worth making accommodations for to be able to benefit from his presence, ideas, problem-solving ability and experience in the workplace.

HR Accommodations

Accommodations here should be read alongside those in the ADHD chapter; there are many similarities. The main ones suggested by Roberto include:

- With the person's permission, inform the line manager, first aiders and MHFAs how rejection affects your RSD colleague, what they should be aware of and how to help diffuse a situation.
- If your colleague is getting overemotional or showing signs of distress, defuse the situation by taking them out of the work environment and stay with them until they have rationalised events. A good cue for this would be to say 'Let's go for a walk and chat about this'. Roberto's favourite code is a quote from The Prodigy: 'I hear thunder'. He instantly knows that he needs to break away.
- Consider facilitating learning about emotions for your colleague and for other team members (Roberto recommends Plutchik's Wheel of Emotions, which helped him 'step outside of himself and look in'). He suggests that it will work out at the same cost as providing a ramp for a wheelchair and offer the same benefit of being able to be more productive all around.
- In meetings, deliberately seek the views of the person with RSD (and/or ADHD). Give them time to respond. Listen, show that you have heard what they have said and thank them for their contribution. You may be pleasantly surprised by the ideas and solutions that they have (but are otherwise afraid to state for fear of rejection).
- Don't surprise RSD/ADHD colleagues. It's always best to advise them in advance of changes that are occurring so that they have time to adjust, understand that it is not a personal slight against them, and prepare their considered (rather than emotional) questions. RSD/ADHD people can have high levels of mutual trust with colleagues and bosses. It is highly unlikely they will 'spill the beans' in advance, divulging sensitive information before a meeting or event.
- Don't put someone like this in the middle of an open-plan office; find an edge or a window where they can concentrate on their work without feeling they are at the centre of attention.

- Allow the use of headphones and music whilst working in an open-plan office, but better still, allow them to work from home when a big project needs completing on time.
- Plan feedback carefully. Whilst many people in the workplace prefer to be told straight out that they have made a mess of something or failed in a project, people with RSD need to be helped to understand what went well and to learn for themselves why it might not be considered to have met the brief. The following coaching style is needed: 'What went well?', 'Tell me about the things that you would do differently', 'What have you learned?', 'What would you suggest as the way forward?', 'How should we explain this to our Exec team?' Ensure that you praise the ideas, the things that went well and the progress that has been made.

Further Resources
https://www.adhdunlocked.co.uk/blog/2020/11/03/elementor-1456/

https://www.psychologytoday.com/us/blog/friendship-20/201907/what-is-rejection-sensitive-dysphoria

https://edgefoundation.org/can-the-pandemic-heighten-rejection-sensitivity-dysphoria/

See Also
Attention Deficit Hyperactivity Disorder (ADHD)

Highly Sensitive Person (HSP) aka Sensory Processing Sensitivity (SPS)

53

Rheumatoid Arthritis (RA)

Mariana was a competitive rower. When she first started to get pain in her feet and knees, she visited a sports physio, who suggested that she try some insoles in her shoes and some fitness routines to get her back into shape. She carried on rowing through the pain for some time, up to the point where her feet and hands were so swollen that a different physio questioned whether she had an inflammatory disease. She suggested that she get referred by her GP for blood tests, and once they were back, the GP fast tracked her to a rheumatology consultant.

At this point, Mariana was in her early thirties, the classic age that people are diagnosed with rheumatoid arthritis. The disease had got a grip on her. Her sleep was affected, and she couldn't walk without pain. The initial consultant wasn't ready to take action and simply wanted her to undertake further exercise and physio and go for some scans.

When she met the NHS-appointed physio, Mariana was in tears with the pain. He emailed a different consultant, explaining the state Mariana was in, and that she was fit and young and in real pain. The new consultant agreed to see her before her other patients the following morning.

The new consultant recognised Mariana's distress and administered an injection of Kenalog, a steroid given to reduce inflammation, together with Hydroxychloroquine and Methotrexate tablets. Over the next twelve weeks, she received two further steroid injections whilst the drugs started to work, with regular blood tests to monitor their impact.

To get some relief from the treatment regime and the loss of her three joys in life – rowing, running and walking up hills – she went out to Majorca but learned the hard way that RA thrives on humidity. Whilst dry heat works well, a steam room or humid heat does not.

Later, when Mariana returned to England from her secondment in Scotland, it took a staggering eighteen months to get her new care plan in place. Everything had to be restarted due to the differences between the two systems. During this period, she was getting flare-ups with the disease, sometimes brought on by heavy rainfall and the subsequent humidity that went with it. She had already decided to wean herself off Methotrexate, which was the cause of mouth sores, skin infections, keratitis (inflammation of the cornea), and she was noticing that some of her hair was falling out. In addition, she was fatigued continuously (the kind of tiredness that is not relieved by sleep), and her brain was foggy.

Finally, she met her new consultant and landed on her feet. Here was a woman prepared to fast track her through the various medicines that had already failed her. She found an opportunity to try some of the newer biological products with her. The first was Benepali, a drug that has to be injected into subcutaneous fat (stomach, arms, thighs) every week. It worked well for the first year before the symptoms started to return, as her body began to build up antibodies against the medicine. Mariana also noticed a rash and some lumps on her fingers, which she was able to self-diagnose as drug-induced lupus (confirmed later through blood tests). Consequently, she had to come off Benepali and suffered another flare-up, with pain and swelling being the main issues.

Mariana is currently awaiting the opportunity (slowed up by the pandemic) to try Abatacept. This is an immunomodulator that blocks T-cell activity and might work as soon as two weeks after first taking it or as long as six months.

Each new drug brings with it a mix of emotions. Hope that arthritis will be put in abeyance, alongside fear that it will either not work at all or create side effects that are even worse than the original condition. After all, these medicines have health warnings associated with them, not dissimilar to chemotherapy drugs.

Given that Abatacept may also have a limited lifespan before she has to set it aside, Mariana has started studying the possibilities of mixing Eastern and Western medicine at the next stage. Native Americans have used *Echinacea pallida* roots; in Uruguay, the dried leaf of ivy (*Hedera helix*) is prescribed; and in China, *Tripterygium wilfordii* is preferred. Mariana notes that pregnant women report that their symptoms disappear during their term; maybe there is a link to the hormones or similar that will be researched. This chapter is not suggesting that any reader should try these, just that keeping an open mind to other cultures is sometimes a good idea.

As well as avoiding humidity, Mariana avoids a range of foods that lead to flare-ups: trans fats, gluten, refined carbs, white sugar, nuts, beans, citrus fruits, garlic and onions. She is also aware that stress and anxiety can bring on a flare-up.

HR Accommodations

RA can be considered a hidden condition as sufferers may well appear fit and healthy. Mariana suggests the following tips for the work environment:

- When a colleague tells you they have rheumatoid arthritis, find time to listen and discover how it affects them. There are many common symptoms, but some will be unique to that person.
- If they have just been diagnosed, ensure they have access to counselling support. It can be daunting to discover that you have a degenerative disease, whatever age you are diagnosed.
- If a major change is planned, reduce the individual's stress by warning them about it in advance.
- Ask your IT team to provide a range of tech solutions. These might include modified keyboards and mice, recording input devices and software and other items as needed.

- Offer flexible hours. If there is a flare-up, the person may need to switch their working hours. Mornings can be difficult if exercises are needed to reduce the pain and swelling before starting.
- Find ways to measure the person on their output, not their hours worked.
- Always remember that they could be hiding pain and putting on a brave face on the days that they might look well.

Further Resources
https://www.arthritis.org/
https://nras.org.uk/
https://www.versusarthritis.org/

54

Sleep Apnoea

When I briefed Ismail on the nature of this book, his first thought was that sleep apnoea wasn't worthy of inclusion. He felt that it had a limited impact at work and might be better dismissed. It is my belief that this hidden condition is worthy of a short chapter at least, if for no other reason than to help those who have not come across it to understand it better, and so I persuaded him to complete our conversation.

Ismail was first made aware that he had an issue when his partner shook him awake late one night, fearing he might have died in his sleep. Apparently, he had been snoring loudly and rhythmically and then suddenly fell completely silent. This repeated several times after the initial event, and his partner searched online the following morning to discover the cause (having himself not slept a wink).

A couple of weeks later, Ismail was wearing a face mask linked to a continuous positive airway pressure machine (CPAP), whilst he had small electrodes stuck to his chest, as the respiratory team at his local hospital monitored what was happening.

They diagnosed obstructive sleep apnoea, a condition where tissue in the throat relaxes and blocks the airways, preventing normal breathing when asleep. It is a condition made worse by people who sleep on their backs, something Ismail was fond of, and is sometimes linked to people who are overweight, drink a lot of alcohol or smoke.

It can be cured in some patients by diet and exercise, by surgical removal of the excess tissue in the throat, by the insertion of a mouth guard at night (which creates a space), but more commonly, it is resolved by the loan of a CPAP machine. The machine produces a steady stream of filtered air through a mask that covers the nose and mouth, forcing the airway open so that breathing whilst asleep remains uninterrupted.

Why does sleep apnoea need to be treated? It is not simply about allowing the partner or other family members to sleep undisturbed; the issue is that the brain is denied oxygenated blood when the breathing rhythm is interrupted. This leads to tiredness during the day as well as an increased risk of high blood pressure and strokes if not treated.

When he reflected on his diagnosis, Ismail recognised that tiredness at work had been commented upon by his assistant, who had joked that he often seemed to need a nap during the day as he got older. He was also aware that he had struggled to stay awake whilst driving between company sites, and now he knew the reason why.

Ismail now has a CPAP machine set up at home and an extra lightweight version to take with him when travelling. He explains that as long as he uses it at night, he can get through a day without feeling tired and that it has made a huge difference. When travelling, he has to wake up a bit earlier than colleagues so that he doesn't scare them at breakfast – because it is tightly fitted, the face mask makes indentations on his forehead and cheeks that he needs to massage out – but other than that he has no issues.

HR Accommodations

Ismail suggests that if an employee lets you know that they have been diagnosed with sleep apnoea that you listen to how it affects them and make any necessary changes that are needed. These might include less driving on company business and ensuring an additional baggage allowance for economy flights (since he needs to take his CPAP machine with him whenever he sleeps overnight). He has been advised not to drink alcohol at night or smoke, but neither of these is an issue. Time off will be needed for annual outpatient visits, where he is tested and reviewed and the machine is serviced, but otherwise, there should be a limited impact.

Further Resources

https://sleep-apnoea-trust.org/
https://www.hope2sleep.co.uk/

55

Stillbirth

Stillbirth (after twenty-four weeks of pregnancy) and miscarriage (before twenty-four weeks of pregnancy) both involve the loss of a baby. Both are devastating to the mother and partner. Both can give rise to a deep sense of loss, feelings of failure and guilt, loss of confidence, anxiety, catastrophising future chances of parenthood, fatigue, brain fog and blood pressure, to name just a few. A stillbirth occurs in around one in every two hundred pregnancies, and a quarter of all pregnancies result in miscarriage. When someone has the courage to tell you about their loss, stop everything else you are doing and give them the time they need, and then think through what will be needed to support them. What you do in these circumstances may well reflect on both you and your organisation for decades to come.

Whilst the majority of this book is based on interviews, Sarah Jones chose to write her own chapter. It reads well, it comes from the heart, and it includes some valuable lessons for us all. Over to Sarah:

2020, the year of the pandemic, also saw the introduction of statutory bereavement leave for parents. A guarantee of two weeks statutory minimum pay when you lose your child. Great.

Speaking from personal experience, when you have lost a child and your whole world has fallen apart, when you barely know how to function, how to live, two weeks seems an insult.

It offers a guarantee, a safeguard for finances, but as an employee suffering a bereavement, it's unlikely to ever be enough.

Employers should consider throwing away the rule book completely: no policy, procedure, rule or expected behaviours will ever teach you how to handle a bereaved employee. It is essential to put the human back into human resources. Professionally, we are trained to follow the rules, the policy, follow things to the letter, be risk averse – but the greatest risk here is doing exactly that.

Everyone will deal with loss differently; some will opt to come back to work quickly, for distraction, for the comfort of people, for avoidance, to ease the pain. Others will need more time. I needed more time and therefore used maternity leave at the time of my loss.

I was off for almost six months, and the first four spent barely surviving day-to-day. I was lucky enough to have a close friend at work, a buddy, someone who dealt with the updates for me, someone who would talk to me as a friend but also communicate my needs to my employer. Someone who helped me return to work – I'm not sure if I'd have been able to do it without her.

Communication was sent to my colleagues with my permission, and this was extremely important. It meant that when I returned, only one person asked me how the baby was and how I was coping at night-time: there were sleepless nights for sure, but sadly not for the reason intended by the questioner. He had clearly missed or forgotten the communication and assumed that I'd been off on regular maternity leave. Perhaps an update close to my return might have helped?

A meeting before I returned also helped. It was a chance to take that first step back into the building. My 'buddy', and close friend, met me in the car park. She was allowed time to attend the meeting with me – also important as I could barely take in anything that was said.

A pattern of hours and a return-to-work date were agreed upon, and this was reviewed weekly. I recall not even being able to type my name when I first sat down at my computer. It helps not to be left alone when you are first back, and a buddy system really makes a difference.

Before my loss, I worked in a customer-facing role. I knew I wouldn't be able to face customers when I returned, and thankfully my employer agreed for me to work in the back office in a new team as part of my phased return.

There were benefits and drawbacks to this. The benefits were that I wasn't in a customer-facing role, and I was in a new team that hadn't been through my journey of pregnancy. The drawback: I was in a new team I didn't know; I didn't have the comfort blanket of my former colleagues and friends.

The learning from this would have been to have better integration between me as the employee suffering the bereavement and my substantive team. Catch-ups, one-to-ones with team members, interaction with my substantive manager – these all stopped when I was posted in my temporary role as a temporary adjustment. Eventually, I moved into a new team, a new change in career direction at a time I was most vulnerable. I'm not sure if it was a blessing or a curse, but nevertheless, it got me into HR!

Even so, in hindsight, I feel it would have been beneficial to have that integration, to not feel outcast due to losing my child. You suffer guilt enough for that without feeling excluded. Who knows? I might have returned to my substantive role in time if that was the case.

This is purely an observation for businesses to consider. Some businesses may not consider such an adjustment as moving teams at all, but they should. The employee needs time, and the more an organisation supports and works with an employee, the better engaged they will be, the more they will value their organisation and eventually, when things become easier, the more productive they will become. They will remember how you responded at that moment forever – not the things that are happening now or that happened before – that moment of return.

It is so much more than just pay, statutory pay at that. Employers have an opportunity to make a real difference to their employees, regardless of the type of bereavement, and by doing so, they are likely to get their employees back to full capacity sooner than an employee who is forced to return early and is resentful of the way they are treated.

It comes back to the fact that everyone deals with bereavement differently and the absolute bread and butter of the situation is open communi-

cation: to never assume as an organisation that you know what is best for the employee; and to really understand and work with their needs within the parameters of the business. That will be a business that is remembered forever as a supportive business and as a good place to work, particularly in times of crisis.

You are probably reading this reaching out for guidance because it is so unknown; I would reiterate to please throw away the rule book and just be human. You will be remembered forever in the most positive way.

HR Accommodations
Our learnings from Sarah's experience are:

- Communications are key. Keep in touch, let the team know what has happened.
- Having a buddy can be a lifeline.
- Consideration for suitable alternative work should be given, especially when the original role is customer-facing, but communications with the original team need to be maintained.
- Throw out the legal minimum: a mother who has experienced a stillbirth won't necessarily bounce back after two weeks. Talk to them, see where you can help, be flexible and supportive.
- Everyone is different. Don't assume that an experience supporting one person through bereavement will be the same as another. Some will want the distraction of work; others won't be able to face it straight away.
- A gentle return mechanism may help, e.g. a meeting before the first day back, being accompanied by a buddy on return or at meetings.
- Remember that items discussed at meetings probably need to be followed up with an email to confirm. With so much going on in their head, not everything will be taken in or processed.
- Some people catastrophise an event such as a stillbirth; professional counselling can help.

Further Resources

https://www.tommys.org/baby-loss-support
https://www.miscarriageassociation.org.uk/
https://babyloss-awareness.org/organisations/

See Also

Miscarriage

56

Sudden Loss (Bereavement)

On 14th October, Nicky's sister died from cancer a year after being diagnosed. Whilst still on bereavement leave and trying to sort things out, Nicky's husband died suddenly of heart failure on 29th October. Nicky had two children (two and ten years old), a full-time job and she now knew she was carrying the deadly BRCA1 gene that gave her an eighty-five per cent chance of developing breast or ovarian cancer. She knew that for the sake of her children, she would need to have her ovaries and fallopian tubes removed, together with a double mastectomy.

This is the very moment that the HR team needs to throw away the bereavement and sick-pay policies and find the most supportive way forward. Whilst the person has not been diagnosed with a hidden disability or condition, you could find that they quickly develop a condition if not supported.

In talking about her experiences, Nicky explains that the most difficult thing was meeting other people. No one knew what to say; they were embarrassed and mumbled words like, 'I can't imagine what you're going through'. She needed someone to let her take the lead and ask for help as issues arose or emotions came to the surface. She needed practical help with making arrangements for the funeral and wake whilst awaiting the autopsy, sorting out probate, resolving banking issues and helping the children understand what had happened.

Everyone handles sudden loss like this in their own way. Some people need the distraction of work; others need time to grieve at home with their family and friends. As an employer, you need to be ready to respond and remain flexible at such times, ensuring that cover for the role is provided without making the person feel that their job is under threat. The last thing they need is the additional stress of fighting for time off.

Nicky had the good fortune to know the founder of Grief Encounter. The counselling support and help that she and her daughters received was key to finding a way through the maze of sudden loss. In Nicky's case, she chose this route. Meanwhile, many GPs will offer medicines to help control anxiety, stress, lack of sleep or depression, but often counselling and techniques such as CBT and Mindfulness can be just as effective.

HR Accommodations

Nicky suggests that HR teams think about the following things when supporting someone who has just suffered a sudden loss:

- There are no right or wrong things to say; the important thing is to start a dialogue, offering practical support where you can. Talk normally, don't tilt your head to one side, speak slowly or in a patronising voice, and avoid saying things like 'It must be terrible for you'.
- Be led by the bereaved person, but keep checking in.
- Ask open questions such as 'What do you need?' and avoid, 'When can you come back to work?' in the early stages.
- The current legal position in the UK (2021) is that an employee can take up to two weeks' bereavement leave for the death of a child and 'reasonable' time off for the death of a close family member. There is no right to paid leave, but please be as generous as you can; it will be repaid over and over again in the future, and provide paid compassionate leave, mixed with the use of annual paid leave if needed.
- If you have an occupational health team, suggest that they provide support and help find suitable counselling if the GP is unable

to (budgets are limited and generic counselling is very different to specialist bereavement counselling).

- Talk to your MHFAs about bereavement and the impact it can have. Typically, the training doesn't cover it (even though it is far more common than psychosis or drug addiction in the workplace), and it's helpful if it is understood.

Further Resources
www.cruse.org.uk/
www.griefencounter.org.uk/
www.mind.org.uk/information-support/guides-to-support-and-services/bereavement/about-bereavement/
www.mariecurie.org.uk/help/support/support-directory/bereavement-and-funerals

See Also
Breast Cancer
Death of a Young Child

57

Tourette Syndrome and Tics

Tics are sudden repeated twitches, movements or sounds that are made by a person without being able to control them. They include motor tics, which might exist as a hand or arm movement or something like repeated blinking, and vocal tics, where they might make a grunting sound, a humming noise or a clicking in their throat.

Some people have one tic that they live with; others have several. Although medical diagnosis varies around the world, it is generally accepted that Tourette syndrome is diagnosed when a person has two or more motor tics and at least one vocal tic that continue for several months or more.

Tourette syndrome is a complex disorder that is probably caused by a combination of genetic and environmental factors. Males are diagnosed at a rate three or four times higher than females in the USA, where the majority of the data has been researched. Researchers are studying the effects of dopamine, serotonin and other neurotransmitters; they are using flashing lights as triggers and taking complex brain traces to understand signalling activity, but at this stage, it is still relatively unknown and a developing research field.

People with Tourette syndrome mostly lead healthy, active lives but can struggle in new environments as people get used to their tics. And, as popularised by some reality TV shows, some people are far more vocal, and their tic includes the use of foul or abusive language, shouted out loud (usually to the room, not to another individual). This is called coprolalia and affects around one in ten people with Tourette syndrome.

Co-morbidities include Attention Deficit Hyperactivity Disorder (ADHD), anger management issues, autism, Obsessive-Compulsive Disorder (OCD), depression, learning difficulties and sleep, anxiety disorders and pain due to the tics.

Olivia has a number of tics, which come and go at different times. She makes a clicking sound with her tongue and often clears her throat; she hums; she keeps biting and banging her teeth together; she stretches her arms out in front of her until her elbow clicks; she sucks her stomach in until her bones are visible and then inflates until it looks like a balloon; she scrunches up her eyes and she makes a range of noises when she is asleep (helping us understand that this is an involuntary act). All of the above occur both with others and when there is no one else in the room to witness it. Some people with Tourette syndrome can suppress actions, heightening the intensity of the tics when they are feeling more comfortable to let them out. This ability to suppress means that for some the condition is hidden in their workplace. The downside is that suppression in itself can be exhausting and lead to fatigue.

During the pandemic, Olivia has been asked to leave her class on several occasions because others are concerned that her regular throat clearance and nervous cough might be the first signs of Covid. She can sometimes be distracted by engaging in a conversation or other activity which requires concentration, and clearly isn't aware that she is performing the tics. The good news for Olivia is that she doesn't shout out and certainly doesn't shout profanities or abuse.

Olivia has taken medical advice to try to reduce the tics. She maintains a low-sugar diet, she takes a magnesium supplement and tries to keep screen time to a minimum (not easy in a pandemic).

There is no cure for Tourette syndrome, but two types of behavioural therapy have been shown to reduce tics in some patients. The first is known as habit reversal training, in which the feelings that trigger tics are ascertained, and then a less noticeable way of relieving the urge to tic is introduced. The second is exposure with response prevention (ERP), a method that trains the body to tolerate the feeling of the tic and control it until it passes. With this method, the patient has to learn to recognise the signs that a tic is about to occur, so this is most successful with older patients.

Where a consultant believes that a tic is harming the individual (physically or socially), then medicines might be prescribed. These include a range of drugs that reduce dopamine, but unfortunately, all have side effects and so are not used with children. Botox injections have been used to relieve some vocal tics. ADHD medications appear to reduce tics in some people and enhance them in others: it is clearly an imprecise science very much related to the individual. Blood pressure tablets have reduced some behavioural problems and rage attacks, whilst antidepressants have reduced anxiety and OCD. And finally, some recent studies suggest that Topiramate, which is normally used to treat epilepsy, might reduce tics. Watch this space.

For anyone reading this as a parent of a young person diagnosed with tics or Tourette syndrome, it is worth noting that the symptoms start reducing after puberty and completely disappear for about a quarter of all teenage patients by the time they reach their twenties. Tim Howard, who played as a goalkeeper for Manchester United and Everton, was ridiculed at school for his tics, but he practised all the behavioural training that was given to him and learned how to suppress the condition.

HR Accommodations

In the workplace, the following accommodations are suggested:

- If an interview candidate tells you that they have Tourette syndrome, ask what the nature of the tics are. Explain to the panel so that they have time to adjust and be ready. Stress can exacerbate tics, and tics can be quite tiring. Allow some extra time for the interview and proper breaks if it is going to take place over a longer period of time.

- Ask for support from an occupational health specialist to review any possible issues if motor tics could create potential issues in the work environment. Hold a small budget for any changes needed.
- On the first day of work, seek permission to introduce the person to their new work colleagues one by one, where possible. Many Tourette syndrome people find large group meetings difficult if they are still learning how to suppress their tics. Allow extra breaks.
- Many people with Tourette syndrome have special skills or knowledge that is unique to them. Work with them to find what their skills are and then find ways to give them plenty of opportunities to use them.
- Tics will come and go but will probably be worst in the first few weeks when everything is new. Continue to help them through this period, and you will have an excellent new team member.

Further Resources
https://www.tourettes-action.org.uk/
https://www.touretteshero.com/
https://www.thebraincharity.org.uk/

58

Ulcerative Colitis (with reference to Crohn's Disease)

Ulcerative Colitis is a chronic disease that affects the large intestine. It is believed that the body's immune system turns on itself in the colon. The lining becomes inflamed, ulcers develop and the affected person will see traces of blood, mucus and/or pus in their stools, which usually take the form of diarrhoea. Whilst this is hidden to others in the workplace, sometimes there are accompanying symptoms, such as mouth ulcers, painful joints, red eyes and patches of swollen skin that may be noticed. Over time someone with this condition may also experience weight loss as a direct consequence of food stuffs passing so quickly through the body. Flare-ups are often triggered by particular foods. Each person with ulcerative colitis has to learn what their triggers are by a process of elimination in their diet.

Claire-Louise was hospitalised for a year: that is how seriously this condition can affect someone. She first started to experience symptoms long before she was formally diagnosed. Possibly triggered by a divorce, becoming a single mother to two young children, a genetic link, stress or a combination of all the above, Claire-Louise started to get pains in her stomach and the feeling that she really needed the toilet, even when she didn't. She describes the pains as being like hunger. She started passing blood in her stools but chose to ignore it for a while.

When she did raise the issues with her GP, she was referred to a consultant, who quickly diagnosed colitis. She was put on a course of medicines, which certainly helped, but they couldn't control the occasional flare-ups that she had, mostly without any rhyme or reason. In 2017 things became worse, but she soldiered on at work. Her boss was demanding, and there was a lot to do. By now, she was losing a lot of blood and was becoming tired to the point where she would go out to her car for short naps before returning to work.

One day a member of her team challenged her, asking what was happening. She realised that things must have become quite bad for them to have noticed, and she was admitted to the hospital, where they had to perform a blood transfusion. Things became more complicated when Claire-Louise contracted MRSA in the hospital, on top of the added complication of pyoderma (a rare and little understood flesh-destroying condition). One of the treatments given to her resulted in an allergic reaction, and she had to be transferred to another specialist regional hospital where lifesaving re-oxygenation treatments saved her life. She explains that her blood oxygen levels were the lowest the team had ever seen in a living person; she developed euphoria and started laughing at everything the nurses did and said.

Thankfully, Claire-Louise recovered and was able to start a six-week phase back into work, arranged with Occupational Health. Even then, she still had flare-ups, meaning that she sometimes needed the toilet as many as fifty times a day. She learned how to tell her colleagues and manager, and today if she moves teams, she will hand out leaflets explaining her condition. Talking about bowels is not everyone's cup of tea, but it needs to be done, so there is understanding, and others don't assume that she is shirking work or being a nuisance by leaving the meeting midway through a presentation.

Claire-Louise has had to shield during the pandemic. Unfortunately, one of the side effects of the drug (azathioprine) that she has to take to manage the colitis leaves her immunocompromised. It works by stopping the body from attacking itself, but this also stops the body from attacking bacteria and viruses. People taking these drugs have to steer clear of anyone with shingles and they are susceptible to any normal winter cold or bug floating around the office.

Ulcerative colitis affects only the large intestine. Crohn's disease has many similarities, but inflammation can appear anywhere in the digestive tract, from the mouth to the anus. At times doctors will not know exactly which condition a person has and will prescribe medication for irritable bowel syndrome (IBS) in the early stages.

HR Accommodations

Claire-Louise suggests the following accommodations at work:

- Everyone is affected in different ways by colitis, and flare-ups can happen at any time. Have a confidential chat with the person and be led by them in terms of the support they need.
- Try to provide as much flexibility in the working day as possible and find ways to make working at home possible, especially when winter colds are rife or a flare-up has set in.
- Try to respect and maintain the dignity of the person. Bowels will never be an easy subject to discuss, but a certain level of knowledge and empathy will be key.
- Try to position their work area close to the nearest toilets. Provide them with a key and priority access to the disabled loos; sometimes, they will literally not be able to wait for a cubicle to come free.
- Provide extra locker space for a change of clothes in case an accident happens. Consider putting that locker inside the disabled toilet if there is space.
- Ensure there is a working emergency cord in the disabled toilet, just in case the person is taken very ill.
- Some colleagues will suffer from fatigue and need extra rest breaks or to stagger their working day. This is often the case with those who have had bowel resection surgery with Crohn's, as a consequence of the body absorbing fewer nutrients.

Further Resources

https://www.crohnscolitisfoundation.org/what-is-ulcerative-colitis
https://www.crohnsandcolitis.org.uk/

59

Usher Syndrome

Usher syndrome is a genetic disorder that develops at different rates in the womb and after that in the child and adult. Type 1 is defined as a person who is profoundly deaf, loses their vision in their early years and has balance issues; Type 2 people have some hearing loss, which rarely degrades, and gradual sight loss; whilst Type 3 people develop hearing loss and sometimes have balance issues, but normally keep good sight. These three types all relate to specific genetic variations, for which there is currently no cure.

Marc suffers from Type 2 Usher syndrome. He was born partially deaf, but his doctor didn't recognise this because Marc had learned to lip-read from an early age. Marc has his mum to thank for this: she worked tirelessly to help him pronounce words correctly, and it is clear that they must have been a great team. Marc's case is the very definition of a 'hidden' condition; in our Zoom interview for this book, I had no clue that his hearing was anything other than normal, and his diction is way better than mine.

In the classroom, Marc encountered greater problems. He could lip-read a teacher who was standing at the front of the class, so he sat at the front to better understand. But he couldn't always pick up everything said in bigger gatherings, such as the chatter of his friends, and so he occasionally wore hearing aids, which he really didn't like.

Marc did well at school and went on to study biochemistry at university. In the first year there, he saw an optician for a review of his eyesight and mentioned that he was going night blind. He was referred to a consultant and was shocked to learn that he would become blind but that it could take between six weeks and sixty years. He chose to be as positive as he could, graduated, and got a job in a hospital microbiology lab. After a while, he realised that he couldn't read the slides under the microscope, and so, undeterred, he retrained as a teacher.

Teaching went well for sixteen years, up to the point that a difficult year group moved through the school. In Marc's case, they would throw things across the room, knowing that his sight was poor and he wouldn't be able to identify the culprit. Things weren't made any easier by the deputy head, who insisted on handing out papers for Head of Department meetings at the very last minute, as they walked into the room, giving Marc no chance to read them. By now, he needed either assistive equipment or for the notes to be in electronic format.

Marc moved on and worked once more with the NHS, developing award-winning training programmes as new IT systems were rolled out across his county, then in a wider Education, Training and Development role across two counties. Going blind has meant that Marc can't lipread anymore. He says that dual sensory loss is more than twice the loss of one sense. Eventually, he had to take ill-health early retirement, something he is grateful for, as it allows him to undertake a range of voluntary and other work.

HR Accommodations

Today Marc marvels at the work that goes into developing an independent educational plan for a child or staff member with a disability or other requirements, and contrasts that with the complete lack of care that was afforded to him in the work environment.

Marc recommends a number of accommodations that organisations can make to support someone with Usher syndrome in the work environment:

- Involve IT as soon as possible. Ask them to meet the person and discuss what works well for them. For many years Marc used

Dolphin SuperNova, a screen magnifier, but it ran into issues as Windows kept upgrading. Now Marc prefers Apple products, which allow him to zoom in, invert, magnify and verbally interact, alongside the huge benefit of upgrading seamlessly. If your person needs a Mac to do their job, take the fight to the top of IT to get it sorted!

- iPads have been a huge boon: easy to transport, easy to operate, great zoom and inversion technology, way ahead of other products and seamless software upgrading.
- Consider providing products such as: Seeing AI, an app that can tell your colleague what a room contains, identify people and objects, and read bar codes; OrCam MyEye, a wearable device a bit like Google Glass that helps with facial recognition as well as reading text; and Alexa or Google Assist for helping with simple tasks in the workplace. Hearing loops in meeting rooms can also help, but only if you know who the people are and who is speaking.
- Allow the person to choose where they sit in a meeting. Marc sits with his back to the window so that he can see and hear as many people as possible.
- Send copies of presentations to your colleague in advance of the meeting so that they can be magnified or listened to in advance. If you use lots of graphics, please provide a summary of what they show.
- Most of all, Marc reminds us that we need to see the person as a unique asset, someone to enjoy interacting with, and not view them as a legal case waiting to happen!

Further Resources
https://www.usher-syndrome.org/
https://www.microsoft.com/en-us/ai/seeing-ai
https://www.orcam.com/en/blog/taking-chance-technology-story-marc-bilton/

https://www.sense.org.uk/get-support/information-and-advice/conditions/usher-syndrome/

See Also
Blindness and Vision Loss

60

Vertigo or Vestibular Dysfunction

In popular parlance, vertigo is used by people who have a fear of heights when they look over the ground far below. In actuality, acrophobia is the fear of heights; vertigo is merely the symptom of that fear. It is a temporary condition that either resolves itself within a few seconds (when they walk away from the edge) or a few days if it is related to something they have eaten, drunk or is a result of a viral or bacterial infection. But for a small number, vertigo is something that they have to live with, day in and day out. There is no instant fix or cure, and the effects are hidden from the rest of the world.

Vertigo is a symptom with a cause, and there are many causes. Simply put, vertigo is the sensation of spinning whilst standing still. This can be debilitating to varying intensities and accompanied by other symptoms, depending on the cause.

Many of you will have experienced it on a low level before, maybe when standing up too quickly, turning around or bending over, or perhaps when you have had an inner ear infection.

Vertigo is commonly linked to the balance or vestibular system in your body. This system consists not only of your ears but your eyes (and how they perceive things), your brain (how it understands things) and randomly, the soles of your feet (how you feel something). If one of these four components is influencing vertigo, the other three will work harder to compensate so that you can continue to function. However, when experiencing a bad episode of vertigo, this overcompensation mode can make you very tired, and sleep is often the solution.

Sometimes food or drink can trigger vertigo. Foods or drinks high in a chemical called Tyramine can be a trigger because they are high in amino acids. Chicken liver, red meats, yoghurt, chocolate, citrus fruits, nuts, bananas, smoked meats and red wine all contain Tyramine and removal or at least reduction from your diet can help control this. Tyramine and the chemical reaction it has on the body cause blood vessels to dilate, which will cause migraine, and this can induce vertigo too, and you could then have migraine-induced vertigo.

Many people with significant vertigo symptoms will avoid alcohol, not only because it will heighten vertigo but because it causes dehydration, another trigger.

Muhammad's Experience

Muhammad's day is at least an hour longer than everyone else's as he travels around the country with a team promoting a new brand. The vast majority of people who encounter him have no idea he suffers from vertigo; it's a truly hidden condition that he has to live with. Whilst many of us have experienced slight dizziness when we first stand after waking (especially after a few drinks the night before), Muhammad gets a full-on, harsh spinning effect. To compensate, he sets his alarm early and spends that first hour of the day slowly moving from horizontal to vertical, undertaking exercises that are designed to realign the crystals in his inner ear.

Muhammad says that he has learned to live with his condition. For example, if he knows there is a meeting at 11 am that he has to attend, he will stand up at 10.55 am and readjust before walking over. During the day, he has to take care when moving to the standing position from being seated, but it is nothing like transferring from horizontal to vertical. He says that he wishes he could sleep upright, but he just can't.

Every month or so, Muhammad feels nauseous when his alarm goes off. He can't predict when it will happen, but he always knows that trouble is in store. The nausea can be overwhelming and often last for four to six hours, wiping out the morning. He sends his manager a text, and his manager knows he probably won't be in until lunchtime but that he will make up his hours over the rest of the week. This means that the HR sickness absence system can be bypassed.

Muhammad lives in London and travels everywhere by public transport. A few months ago, he was headhunted for a new role with a competitor, but had to decline because their city has poor public transport and getting to other parts of the UK would take too long. Staying in London is going to be the way forward. In a social context, Muhammad's team are all ten years younger than him and want to go bowling, drinking, to karaoke or they want to do something on the Thames. All these options are near impossible when you have vertigo. Muhammad is frustrated that sometimes he can't do some simple things that others take for granted, like running for the bus (he has to wave and hope).

Debbie's Experience

Debbie Sillett writes this chapter in her style.

As a young child, I was clingy and would often complain of a 'poorly head'. I would be given some Disprin and left to get on with things. I also took my favourite teddy to school until I was about eight (not the done thing for an eight-year-old); no one really questioned it or tried to discourage it as they just saw it as some comfort. Then one morning, when I was about ten years old, I woke up and it was as if everything had changed.

I felt dizzy and sick. As I struggled to stand up, I realised I had often felt this way before but hadn't really taken it in. I described these sensations to my mum, who was now able to understand how I was feeling. We then put two and two together with my poorly head and realised that these symptoms would take time to dissipate: I couldn't just jump out of bed and get ready for school. It could take anything up to an hour from me waking before the sensations would settle enough to enable me to stand up. So, every morning now began with a routine of gradually putting a second pillow under my head and moving slowly further and further upright and tak-

ing time in between each move to allow things to settle until the sensations stopped and I could get up.

The GP assessed me, took blood samples, and came to no conclusion apart from maybe it was hormonal as I was approaching my teens. We persevered for a while and, each time out of frustration, saw a different GP, to no avail. This was now causing havoc as I left school and secured my first job, and justifying my situation became more and more difficult. We made a last-ditch attempt with the GP, and I saw the original GP again. He couldn't believe I was still experiencing these symptoms so many years later, and he referred me to a specialist for in-depth tests to try and establish the root cause.

Over the next six years, I was passed from pillar to post, prodded and poked, saw neurologists, neuropsychiatrists, psychiatrists (was I making this all up), behavioural specialists and cardiologists. I was treated and medicated for four years for a condition I didn't even have (postural hypertension – low blood pressure causing dizziness). I was then passed off to yet another doctor, this time a cardiologist at St Marys in Paddington, London, and he was about to discharge me as he 'could do no more' for me, when my mum said, 'This won't do. Debbie has suffered for years, is debilitated to the point she cannot work, and you can't do anything? We're not going anywhere till you figure out what's wrong.'

The cardiologist referred me to the National Hospital of Neurology and Neurosurgery in London to Professor Linda Luxon, a neuro-otologist. Her clinic specialises in hearing and balance disorders, and after four hours and six rather nasty investigative procedures, I had a diagnosis with a 100% positive prognosis. It had taken till I was twenty-seven years old, but I finally knew that I had vestibular dysfunction. One of the vestibules inside my left inner ear is damaged. It was damaged from birth, so there was nothing we could have done or known. This causes the left side of my balance system not to function instantly on waking and rising after sleeping, and induces vertigo, light-headedness, room spinning and nausea, all to varying degrees.

Just knowing felt like a massive weight had been lifted off me. At every job, my sickness record had been crazy, and I had been dragged through Occupational Health at every opportunity, but until now, I couldn't justify any of it. I was made to feel like a fake and a liar when this was very real to me.

The consultants were great, and whilst there is no medication, treatment or cure for my condition, they taught me how to live with vertigo. I was taught a set of exercises called Cawthorne-Cooksey, which triggers the symptoms. By performing them daily, my brain retrains itself and learns to cope with vertigo. I was advised that patients with balance disorders will suffer from a sleep disorder, so I undertook a sleep study and was diagnosed with insomnia, the most straightforward of them all, thank goodness. It could have been narcolepsy, parasomnia, sleep apnoea or restless leg syndrome.

I also suffer from another type of vertigo sporadically. This is called Benign Paroxysmal Positional Vertigo (BPPV). As the name suggests, it's related to the position of the body and causes violent dizziness when changing from vertical to horizontal and turning over in the night. So mostly, this affects me during the night and hence has an impact on my sleep pattern. BPPV is the most common type of vertigo, and it's both temporary and treatable. It's caused by 'crystals', or calcium deposits, becoming dislodged and free floating in the vestibules. This is what causes dizziness. Sometimes it will correct itself over time, but nothing I do is ever simple, so back to the neuro-otologist we went. They conducted a procedure called the Epley Manoeuvre, which involves putting the head and body in a sequence of positions to return the crystals to their original position. This can take more than one attempt, but it is a game-changer. Thanks to Google, I found a version of the manoeuvre that you can conduct yourself over several nights before going to bed, and this, slowly but surely, has given me the same result.

HR Accommodations

Debbie and Muhammad suggest the following accommodations should be considered:

- Take time to listen to how vertigo affects them. Whilst many struggle with transitions (e.g. sleeping to waking, horizontal to vertical, seated to standing), others find they have episodes linked to drinking or eating, and some when under stress.
- Suspend any sickness absence systems that trigger with regular short periods of lateness or absence. Be flexible if you can.
- Offer the opportunity to work from home when you can; your colleague will be much more productive.
- Where possible, find alternatives to lifts. Muhammad really struggles with fast lifts in tall buildings.
- Try to be inclusive in social activities – not all the time, but on occasion.

Further Resources

https://www.entuk.org/vertigo

https://www.menieres.org.uk/information-and-support/symptoms-and-conditions/bppv

https://www.brainandspine.org.uk/our-publications/our-factsheets/vestibular-rehabilitation-exercises/

See Also

Ménières Disease

61

Williams Syndrome (WS)

When I first met Anastasia, I had never heard of Williams Syndrome. It is a rare developmental condition that is present in one in about five thousand people, with different levels of impact (about one in ten thousand where it is formally diagnosed). In the literature, there is conjecture about whether it is an inherited condition or results as a consequence of a piece of genetic code being deleted when the sperm fertilises the egg. Typically, people with Williams Syndrome have heart and vascular problems, high calcium levels, sensitive hearing, distinctive facial features, a mix of learning and/or motor skills challenges, attention deficit disorder (ADD) and are likely to suffer bouts of anxiety and depression. These features sit alongside a high-level ability with language, music and rote memory, combined with engaging personalities and an interest in other people.

Born in Hong Kong, Anastasia's first few weeks of life were spent in an incubator as the team helped her make her entry into the world. She travelled with her family to South Africa and Russia before finally settling in the UK. She was aware from an early age that she had Williams Syndrome and remembers being bullied at school because she was different. When I asked her about this, she explained that she had to wear glasses to correct her eyesight and that her motor skills meant that playing ball games in the playground was limited. She also had issues with her speech, which have been completely corrected by speech therapy (there being no hint of an issue during my interview with her). Williams

Syndrome is included in this book because it is not obvious in some of its forms.

Anastasia has a fast metabolism. It means that she can eat as much as she wants and struggles to put on weight. She has been working out at the gym to build and strengthen her upper body, something that the pandemic halted, as she has to take precautions against getting infected with Covid. On a more serious level, she has a heart condition that needed a 'scary' valve repair in 2015, with annual check-ups ever since.

Anastasia has a love of the violin and piano, and she can play music by ear, making her the envy of many, utilising her ability to retain and memorise data. She has played at an advanced level with orchestras, including solos, and can also sing very well. She is bilingual (English and Russian), is exceptionally engaging as a personality, and is mentally strong.

Anastasia has diplomas in animal, child and social care and has worked in a range of different environments. She currently works as a volunteer for Oxfam but will make an excellent store manager when her training is complete (that's if her favourite ice hockey team, the Coventry Blaze, don't hire her to recruit and negotiate contracts with Russian players, of course).

HR Accommodations
Anastasia offers the following advice to employers:

- Learn all about Williams syndrome from the internet and by talking to the person about how it affects them.
- Help educate the team about Williams syndrome. Anastasia finds that talking about it openly builds great team relationships.
- Every person diagnosed with Williams syndrome has a different set of personal characteristics, but typically they are very engaging and, whilst accommodations may need to be made for tasks in-

volving motor skills, you will quickly find that you have a valuable new member of the team.

- Be patient and respectful when initially explaining something, and check for understanding. Allow for attention to drift if the person has associated ADD. But once trained, the person will be very capable.
- Avoid asking someone with Williams syndrome to work in a large, ever-changing project team. Small groups are best, where the person has the chance to develop trusting relationships.
- Illustrations and pictures often work far better than lengthy sentences when explaining something or setting a project.
- Try to minimise changes in routines in the first few months. Allow the person to settle into the new team first.
- Pre-warn colleagues with Williams syndrome when a fire drill is likely to happen and ensure they have a buddy.
- Be clear in all communications. If there is any confusion or ambiguity, then the chances are that they will see it differently to you. So check for understanding after detailing a project or task.
- Try to minimise the use of writing implements. Where fine motor skills are required, use a technology provided by the IT team instead.
- Some people with Williams syndrome suffer from high levels of anxiety. In such cases, it is important to introduce new training or any change with positive re-enforcement rather than negative comments (see the NCBI paper below).

Further Resources
https://williams-syndrome.org/what-is-ws
https://rarediseases.org/rare-diseases/williams-syndrome/
https://www.ncbi.nlm.nih.gov/pmc/articles/PMC5452620/

Conclusion

All organisations need to make appropriate accommodations to help their employees play a full part in society. Many accommodations are generic and provide extra support, flexible working hours being one obvious example. Others are specific to the condition or person and will provide a significant benefit: not just to the individual, but also to their colleagues, who will appreciate what the organisation is doing.

Once you create a more open and inclusive environment, people will feel less of a need to hide their condition(s) and, as a consequence, they will become more productive and quite possibly stay with you for longer.

For a small cost it is a big win-win.

Acknowledgements

The following amazing people gave me their time, energy, inspiration and ideas for the various chapters in the book. Some provided support through their expertise and knowledge; others through their lived experience; many both. Throughout the book, names have been altered to avoid disclosure where it was unwanted.

Davita Akari
Mo Amir
Turvi Apte
Charlotte Baker
Louise Baker
Vicky Bates
Marc Bilton
Kyra Bransom
Joanna Buckard
Anna Butcher
Tim Caisley
Chioma
Kirsty Diamond
Emma
Greig Fairweather
Fiona Findlay
Melanie Francis
Katy Glenn
Enrique Gonzalez
Kathy Greethurst
Claire-Louise Hall
Sarah Hanna
Claire Haskins

Gill Holden
James Holiday-Scott
Iza
Nicola Johnson
Rosin Johnson
Sarah Jones
Benedicta Joppa
José
Kathryn
Eileen Kerr
Anna Kettlewell
Aidan Kiely
Julian King
Nicky Levy
Lisa
Tiffany Lowe
Ashley Loxley
Janet MacKinnon
Alice McEvoy
Julia McFarland
Sarah McGuiness
Danielle McPherson
Mikhail
Tilley Milburn
Natalie Cantorna Miller
Simon Millward
Eleanor Minshall
Yvonne Mitchell
Gemma Morris
Muhammad
Jules Parkinson-Thake
Liz Parr
Phoebe ("To Sue: thank you for sharing your strength, determination
and humour with me")
Hannah Rigby

Jess Rigby
Katharine Rogers
Claire Rooks-Byron
Kate Rotheroe
Steph Sawyers
Olayinka Seriki
Hanah Sfar-Gandoura
Debbie Sillett
Aarin Smith
Alejandra Vargas Sotelo
Nicola Strahan
Anastasia Sutton
Revd Jayne Taylor
Sherry Thompson
Eileen Thornton
Teresa Wilkins
Nicola Winwood
Julie-Ann Wyatt

Many of the connections that I made arose from interactions with the Facebook Group 'HR Ninjas' that has over 15k members, all working in HR and supporting each other. A big thank you to Lizzie Henson and Metra Rowe for their encouragement.

A huge thank you also goes to Laura Matthews at www.barnett-waddingham.co.uk for talking me through all the options for company health care and insurance schemes. Laura is genuinely passionate about employee wellbeing and advises on what is suitable and appropriate depending upon the type and size of an organisation and its employees.

The artwork on the front cover was created by Tilley Milburn (with inspiration provided by Del the Piggie) to express some of the issues faced in a neuro-diverse life: https://www.heartnsoul.co.uk/artists/tilley-milburn.

The illustration inside the book was created by Valentina Rinaldi, who has worked with me on many of my books, especially those written for children: https://www.valeblublu.com/

Editing was in the expert hands of Bryony Sutherland, who did such a great job for me with *Human Resources A to Z*. Editing is not just about spotting my many grammatical and spelling errors; it is about helping develop the initial concept and challenging the structure and style, whilst providing a fresh pair of eyes at the key moments: https://bryonysutherland.com/

Ted Smith is a senior human resource and organisational development consultant, currently working as MD at UKHR.com Ltd. Ted has a degree in environmental science, a diploma in HRM, and has held positions at GlaxoSmithKline, Nielsen, Vernalis, the Medical Research Council and Wellcome Trust. He's worked in Europe, USA, Africa and Asia at executive and board level, and is currently chair of the Ideas Foundation (a charity). Ted is the author of *Human Resources A to Z: A Practical Field Guide for People Managers*, *The Train Blog: Odd and Weird People-Watching*, and has published over a dozen children's stories.

Photo of Ted Smith by Tom Smith.

Lightning Source UK Ltd.
Milton Keynes UK
UKHW020812181121
394190UK00010B/969